CLASSIC
German
RACING MOTORCYCLES

CLASSIC

German

RACING MOTORCYCLES

Mick Walker

OSPREY
AUTOMOTIVE

Page 1
Italian GP, Monza, September 1953. Riders 14, 12, and 52, on works NSUs, get a clean start

Page 2
MZ factory rider Horst Fügner raises spray from his rear wheel during a very wet 125 cc race at the 1957 German GP, Hockenheim

Left
The two-stroke, twin-cylinder Adlers of Hans Hallmeier (114) and Walter Vogel (102) make a sandwich of NSU works rider and World Champion Werner Haas during the 1954 250 cc German GP at Solitude

Published in 1991 by Osprey Publishing
59 Grosvenor Street, London W1X 9DA

British Library Cataloguing in Publication Data

Walker, Mick
    Classic German racing motorcycles.
    1. German motorcycles, history
    I. Title
    629.22750943
    ISBN 1–85532–141–6

Editor Ian Penberthy
Page Design Geoffrey Wadsley

Printed by BAS Printers Limited
Over Wallop, Hampshire
Great Britain

Klaus Enders and Ralf Engelhardt won the sidecar
title a record six times between 1967 and 1974 –
always on BMW machinery

Contents

About the author

Mick Walker is an enthusiast for all forms of motorcycle sport. He has been a successful competitor and has helped many to triumph with his profound knowledge of tuning. There is virtually no aspect of the business in which Mick has not been active at some point, and that includes being an importer of exotic Italian race-bred machines. Today he heads a thriving company that specializes in the supply of spare parts to Ducati owners and racers around the world.

Mick rode a variety of racers during the classic era, including an AJS 7R, Manx Norton, Greeves Silverstone, a brace of BSA Gold Stars, various Ducatis and even 50 and 125 cc Hondas.

Above
The author raced a wide range of bikes over almost a decade, encompassing most of the 1960s. He finally hung up his leathers in 1972

Right
The legendary Nürburgring circuit, a scene during the 350 cc race, German Grand Prix, June 1955

Introduction

In this, the third of the *Classic Racing Motorcycles* series, it is Germany's turn to come under the spotlight. For most of the period covered by this book, there were two distinct Germanys – West and East. Although run under very different political doctrines, they both produced some highly innovative and *competitive* racing machinery.

Not only were German motorcycles often in the very vanguard of technical progress, but they were also good enough to win world titles. In this respect, the top names in the solo categories were NSU and Kreidler, while BMW, Fath, Münch and König did the business on three wheels.

Like the Japanese, the Germans were faced with rebuilding a shattered country following their defeat at the hands of the Allies at the end of World War 2. And like the Japanese, they overcame all the problems not only to create an economic miracle, but also to construct world-beating motorcycles. Much of this success was thanks to Germany's pool of

skilled engineers, both at factory and private level.

There were lone geniuses such as Roland Schnell, Helmut Fath, Gustav Baumm, Dieter König, Friedl Münch and Daniel Zimmermann. At factory level, engineers were actively encouraged to display their skills in their employers' race departments. Among them were Kurt Grasmann and Jan Friedrich Drkosch (Adler), Alex von Falkenhausen (BMW), Erich Wolf and Helmut Görg (DKW), Johannes Hilber (Kreidler), Günther Schier (Maico), Walter Kaaden (MZ), and Albert Roder and Walter Froede (NSU).

These men did not confine their expertise to certain capacity classes, but created racing bikes of all types from 50 cc upwards, together with sidecar machines. In addition, Germany was particularly strong in the record-breaking field, a tradition it had held since the very dawn of motorcycle sporting activities.

Although not so prolific as the British or Italians, German riding talent was also quite effective, particularly in the sidecar field. A short list of German solo stars includes Werner Haas, Hans-Georg Anscheidt, Walter Zeller, Ernst Degner and Dieter Braun. While the names of Wilhelm Noll, Willi Faust, Fritz Hillebrand, Walter Schneider, Helmut Fath, Max Deubel, Klaus Enders and Rolf Steinhausen may not sound as familiar, all had the distinction of winning the world sidecar title at least once – and on German machinery.

Post-war, the Grand Prix was held at five circuits within the German borders. The most famous of these was the Nürburgring, initially the original 14-mile ultra-demanding course, followed later by the shorter South Loop section. Solitude was an extremely picturesque location just outside Stuttgart, now no longer used for racing. The same could be said of the ten-mile Schotten circuit. Used for the national Grand Prix only once, it was viewed by many riders as being positively dangerous.

Sachsenring in the East had been the home of the German GP in pre-war days, and was reintroduced with the advent of a separate East German classic in the early 1960s. Finally, there was the Hockenheim-Ring. Still used today, it is essentially a pair of

Mit herzlichen Grüssen an die Leser

[autographs of various racers including Rupert Hollaus, Geoff Duke, Tommy Wood, Rad Coleman, and others]

Above
*A section of the MZ museum at Augustburg.
Machines are pre-war DKW supercharged two-
strokes*

Left
*NSU works riders Werner Haas and Ruppert Hollaus
head a list of famous names from the Continental
circus of 1954*

straights connected by loops at each end, making the
speed of the machines the dominant factor.

Thus, Germany could be said to have contributed
to the development of the sport in a wide variety of
ways – engineers, machines, riders, circuits, and
even record-breakers. The Germanic motorcycle
racing story has them all, which made this particular
title so interesting to compile.

Many good people helped in some way in the
completion of *Classic German Racing Motorcycles*. As
I have discovered in the past, the vast majority were
only too pleased to provide whatever assistance they
could, and I will always be in their debt.

Unfortunately, the list is almost endless, so I must
apologize to those whose names I have not been able
to mention, but I shall be eternally grateful to them
for the help given.

So I offer acknowledgement to the following, in no
particular order of merit: Brian Woolley, Doug
Jackson, Barry Hickmott, Don Mitchell, John Fern-
ley, Fred Secker, Phil Higston, Emlyn Evans and
Dominique Tellier.

I should also like to make special mention of the
help received from fellow author Alan Cathcart, who
kindly provided additional information on the SMZ
(Maico) twin, raced by Dieter Braun in the early
1970s.

The photographs came from a number of sources,
including Doug Jackson's World Motorcycle News
Agency, Philip Tooth, Len Thorpe, Nick Nicholls,
George Nutall, Alan Kirk, Richard Walker, BMW,
the EMAP archives and my own collection. I have
used as many previously unpublished photographs
as I could, but occasionally it has been necessary to
use a 'familiar' picture due to its historic importance.
As usual, the excellent cover photography is the
work of Don Morley.

I would also record the patience shown by my
dear wife Susan, and the efforts of Kim White, who
typed the manuscript.

Last, but not least, the super-efficient Osprey
editorial team under editor Ian Penberthy, not
forgetting the encouragement provided by Osprey's
editorial manager, Nicholas Collins.

Classic German Racing Motorcycles continues the
review of countries that manufactured racing machines during the 'classic' period, begun with the
British and Japanese. I hope that you will garner as
much pleasure from reading the finished work as I
have had in compiling it.

Mick Walker
Wisbech, Cambridgeshire
June 1990

1
Adler – German eagle

One of Germany's most respected industrial brand names, Adler (Eagle), was not only a pioneer in the manufacture of both cars and motorcycles, but also lives on to this day in the typewriter manufacturing field.

Adler's founder was Heinrich Kleyer, who was born in 1853. His father was a factory owner, and the young Kleyer attended the Darmstadt Technical University. His first job was with an ironware and machinery company in Frankfurt. This was followed by four years in Hamburg with a firm that imported machinery, which led him to go to work in America with the Sturevant Mill Company of Boston.

Heinrich Kleyer returned to Germany in 1886 and founded Adler Fahradwerke AG in Frankfurt am Main. At first, Adler imported American-made pedal cycles, but within a year was manufacturing its own range of bicycles. The period in America had convinced Kleyer of the great potential for future transport requirements, and the business possi-

By 1955 several of the leading privately-tuned Adler twins were watercooled

bilities these offered. His production facilities were housed in a six-storey building (at the time, the highest in Frankfurt), where customers could test the machines on the top floor.

Within a decade, Kleyer's organization had produced its 100,000th bicycle, and in 1898, it came up with the first German-made typewriter. In that year, the company gained the services of Dip. Ing. Franz Starkloph as chief designer and works manager of the Adler bicycle works. Other business ventures at the time included owning the German distribution rights for Dunlop tyres.

In 1898, a licence was also taken out to build French De Dion-Bouton tricyles, but little use was made of this. Instead, Kleyer instructed Starkloph to design a light car powered by a De Dion-Bouton engine. This entered production in 1900. Of more significance to this chapter, however, is the fact that Adler also employed a De Dion engine, a single-cylinder four-stroke, to power its first motorcycle two years later in 1902.

From 1903 onwards, Adler also manufactured its own engines, both single- and twin-cylinder and, again, four-stroke. These early Adler machines were of excellent quality and were also raced in some of the pioneer events, with considerable success, by Kleyer's two sons, Erwin and Otto.

However, Adler, together with many other German motorcycle marques of the era, ceased production at the end of 1907 to concentrate on other (more profitable!) engineering enterprises – in Adler's case, cars, bicycles and typewriters. Furthermore, except for a brief return to powered two-wheelers in 1931, during the worst part of the Depression, when it introduced an engine-assisted bicycle of 74 cc, the Frankfurt company stayed away from motorcycles for some four decades.

The front-wheel-drive Adler Trumpf Junior was one of the most popular German cars of the 1930s, while the company's range of typewriters were market leaders.

However, all had not been as easy as it appeared

A mechanic working on a watercooled Adler 250 at the Nürburgring, August 1955

on the surface. During World War 1, Adler built trucks, transmissions for tanks and aero engines under licence from Daimler-Benz. In 1916, Heinrich Kleyer had taken an interest-free war loan of 4,000,000 reichmarks from the government, but the loan was never repaid fully, the result being that control of the company passed to the Deutsche Bank in 1920. This was because the repayment of the loan was rendered almost worthless by the high inflation which took place within Germany following the end of hostilities.

Fortunately for the Kleyer family, the bankers allowed them to retain managerial control, so the Frankfurt company was able to continue and prosper, avoiding this potential disaster. Shortly after the Trumpf car was introduced in 1932, Heinrich Kleyer died at the age of 79. He was succeeded by his son Erwin, whose interest in streamlining led to some very advanced four-wheel designs during the mid and late 1930s.

With the arrival of World War 2, Adler's production facilities were turned to military requirements once again, in particular staff cars, ambulances and even half-tracked vehicles with Maybach engines.

At the war's end, in the spring of 1945, very little remained of the Adler factories, which were centrally located in Frankfurt, where destruction was around 80 per cent! Somehow, the existing Adler corporate boss, Ernst Hagemeyer, succeeded in setting the wheels in motion to ensure recovery of his shattered empire. It was decided that first typewriter manufacture and then automobile assembly were to be restarted as soon as it was possible to do so.

At first, Hagemeyer envisaged making cars and returning to motorcycle production, for both of which he engaged the services of the talented engineer, Karl Jentschke.

Jentschke was charged with creating a new motorcycle and modernizing the Trumpf Junior car with a 995 cc engine. However, although prototypes appeared, the latter project was soon abandoned. Instead, it was decided to concentrate on the two-wheel venture.

Dieter Falk put up a tremendous performance to finish fifth in the 1958 Isle of Man Lightweight race on his privately-entered, unfaired 250 Adler

First, a new factory was built, its managing director and chief engineer being Herman Friedrich. Initially, it was intended to produce a 60 cc two-stroke commuter machine, as this was the capacity limit imposed on the German manufacturers by the Allied Commission in 1946.

However, by the time production of the new Adler got under way in 1949, these rules had been relaxed. The result was a 98 cc (50 × 50 mm) machine, coded M100.

This first post-war Adler motorcycle was hardly the commercial success that the management team hoped it would be. Even so, it led Friedrich and his engineers to consider other designs, and when the giant Frankfurt Show took place in October 1951, Adlerwerke had three different models to display. These comprised the M100 and its larger brother, the M125, plus a brand-new design, the trend-setting M200 twin. The last machine was to point the way to future Adler developments over the next few years.

This was a much bolder move than may, at first, be appreciated, because, at the time, designing small-capacity two-stroke twins produced a major problem – how to achieve effective crankcase sealing. Friedrich and his engine specialist, Felix Dozekal, came up with a solution that was ingenious, yet complicated.

The two separate crankshafts needed to be located side by side in a common crankcase assembly, the serrated joints of which were held together by a long

To cope with the increase in both power and weight, Adler built a more robust version of the M125 frame. This had plunger rear suspension, while the front forks still retained the 'clock-spring' suspension pioneered on the original M100; 16 in. wheels were specified to provide a low riding position.

Capable of 65 mph, the M200 was well received by both press and customers alike. The influential journal *Das Motoradd* commented: 'a super quality motorcycle in a class of itself; a genuine jewel of German motorcycle production.'

However, the real headline maker was launched in 1953 as the M250. Essentially a larger and improved M200, the new quarter-litre challenger was truly a trend-setting machine, its turbine-smooth engine having equal bore and stroke measurements of 54 × 54 mm and a capacity of 247.3 cc.

The year before, Adler had proved the quality of the twin-cylinder concept when all four of their machines entered in the 27th ISDT in Austria had completed the gruelling rigour of six days in the world's toughest motorcycle test. At the end, they had three golds and a bronze medal to show for their efforts.

This success was instrumental in triggering more competition activity, and soon the first Adler riders began to appear in road races on home-tuned models. Among them were such as Walter Vogel, Willi Bilger, Hubert Luttenberger and the Kramer brothers, Klaus and Ulrich.

However, it was the Nürnburg rider Hans Hallmeier who could claim to have been the first to use a race-kitted M250 twin, which had been tuned by his father. This was in September 1953 in the 20th Eilenriede Rennen held at Hanover. Although the event was won by NSU star and World Champion Werner Haas, it was the Adler twin that commanded the attention of the press boys, not only for its speed, but also its vivid acceleration.

Hallmeier's performance prompted the factory into building a batch of over-the-counter racing models for sale to private customers. These were based on the standard production M250 roadster.

The prototype of the new machine, the RS (Renn Sport), made its début at the Dieburg circuit in the spring of 1954. Its rider was Hubert Luttenberger, who finished this first round of the German national championships in a mid-field position. However, he clearly showed the potential of the newcomer.

Besides its specially-tuned engine, which pumped out a claimed 24 bhp, the most interesting features were the entirely new frame and suspension. These

through-bolt. A roller bearing and a pair of seal rings were housed in the central web of the crankcase. To tighten the through-bolt, a specially-designed tool was inserted through a hole in the offside to locate on a radial serration on the bolt head. The complete crank assembly was supported at both ends in bearing housings which, in turn, were located in the crankcase walls. The cranks were placed at 180 degrees.

With a capacity of 195.4 cc (48 × 48 mm), the M200 employed cast-iron cylinder barrels and alloy heads. These were inclined forward from the vertical by 45 degrees.

The primary drive to the four-speed gearbox was by helical gears. Of particular note was the wet, multi-plate clutch, which was mounted in an outrigger location on the nearside end of the crankshaft.

were the responsibility of Jan Friedrich Drkosch. The frame was neatly crafted from lightweight, aircraft-quality steel tubing, while the suspension featured a swinging arm with pivoted fork at the rear and a pair of hydraulically-damped, leading-link forks up front.

The engine of the RS was largely the work of former aero-engine expert Kurt Grasmann. The same man had developed the M250 power unit for long-distance trials, such as the ISDT, where Adler also enjoyed considerable success.

Grasmann spent a considerable time on the gas-flow characteristics of the Adler twin-cylinder engine, including experimenting with varying inlet and exhaust tract lengths and different expansion chambers. In fact, Adler was carrying out very similar work to that which was being undertaken at the same time by two-stroke rival DKW at Ingolstadt. Both companies were to have a profound influence on the development of the modern two-stroke engine.

The main areas of development undertaken by Grasmann were in the exhaust system, cylinders and

Superbly-drawn illustration of a watercooled Adler RS250, showing the various features of the machine to the best advantage

carburettors. The last were 24 mm Amal TT instruments specially imported from Britain.

Although Adler never officially had a works team, private riders were to achieve some quite outstanding successes over the next few years, both inside Germany and in other countries.

During their first season, the RS Adlers lined up against the all-conquering NSU Rennmax works double-knocker twins. Even so, Hallmeier and Vogel finished third and sixth respectively in the 1954 German GP at Solitude. Moreover, in the Swiss GP at Berne, Vogel repeated the performance with another sixth – excellent results indeed.

The maximum speed of the 1954 RS250 was almost 120 mph, a truly stunning performance for what was, after all, a production-based 250.

By 1955, a handful of the leading Adler tuners had begun to watercool their engines. This was to maintain the optimum power output for a longer period. With the standard aircooled cylinders, the performance would drop as the engine became hotter after a few laps. However, with a water-cooling jacket, the power would remain constant throughout the race. This was particularly important in Grand Prix events which, in some cases, could be of up to three hours in duration.

Watercooling also allowed further tuning to take place. This enabled privately-entered RS250s to give

Englishman Richard Williats rode an Adler with considerable success on British short circuits in the early 1960s. He is pictured here at Castle Coombe in April 1963

race-winning performances throughout the remainder of the 1950s and well into the 1960s.

In fact, some of the best performances by Adlers in road racing came after the factory which had made them ceased production! This was because, from early 1956, the Frankfurt company had found the going ever more difficult, until eventually the giant Gründig electrical empire took over Adler (and also the German Triumph concern) in the winter of 1957–8. However, Gründig had no interest in continuing with the motorcycle side, having taken over the ailing company for its typewriter expertise alone.

Adler had become caught up in the drastic decline in two-wheeler sales which hit Germany in the mid 1950s and led to severe financial crises amongst the vast majority of manufacturers.

However, Adler's fall from grace was not the end of the marque's track successes because, in 1958, Dieter Falk, on a home-tuned RS twin, finished fifth overall in the 250 cc World Championship series. This included a couple of third places at Assen and

the Nürburgring and, perhaps most sensational of all, a magnificent fifth in the Isle of Man TT. Falk was also German champion that year. Günther Beer, on another Adler, also gained some leaderboard placings in the classics during this period.

Tuned by men such as Willi Klee, the final 250 Adlers, in watercooled form, were pumping out 38–40 bhp and could reach almost 140 mph. All this was most impressive, and the potential of the Frankfurt two-strokes was not only realized in Germany itself, but overseas.

In Japan, both Suzuki's and Yamaha's experimental departments imported examples of the M250, and designs such as the Colleda (Suzuki) and the YD1 (Yamaha) owed much to the German machine. In Britain, the Val Page-designed Ariel Leader/Arrow was another machine that borrowed Adler technology.

Even though the German eagle had fallen from grace, its descendants were destined to soar to glories anew.

The Adler was the first really modern two-stroke twin, a type that was to dominate on road and track in the quarter-litre class many years later under the Yamaha badge. This, above all else, is the most fitting tribute to the Adler concept, and is something of which its German creators can be truly proud.

2
BMW solos

The Bayerische Motoren Werke (Bavarian Motor Works) came into existence following a merger, in 1913, between two aero engine manufacturers: the Karl Rapp Motorwerke and the Gustav Otto Flugmotorenfabrik. The new company became the Bayerische Flugzeugwerke in 1916, and BMW the following year.

Both BFW and then BMW were major suppliers of engine units to the German Air Force, and the vital men in the formation of BMW were an Italian-born Austrian banker, Camillo Castiglione, and a young Austrian naval engineer, Franz Josef Popp. The two first came into contact at the Austro-Daimler aircraft engine company. When BMW came into existence on 29 July 1917, Popp was appointed its managing director – a post he was to hold until 1942.

During late 1917 and into 1918, the new company's growth was incredible. It became one of the largest engineering-based companies in Germany which, at its wartime peak, employed over 3500 people. However, when the war finally came to an end in November 1918, its fall was equally spectacular.

After the Armistice, BMW was forbidden to manufacture aero engines, but subsequently it branched out into other fields, including motorcycles.

In 1923, BMW produced its first complete machine, the R32. This had two notable features: shaft drive and a flat-twin engine. Conceived by Max Friz, the 493 cc (68×68 mm) machine was the star of the Paris Show that year and was to influence BMW motorcycle design over the next 60 years.

The first racing BMW was the R37 which, in 1924, with Fritz Bieber at the helm won the German national road-racing title. From then on, for many years, racing was to play an important part in the company's progress.

The R37 had been designed by Rudolf Schleicher, who also rode for BMW in the 1926 ISDT, held in Britain. In this, he gained a gold medal.

In all, BMW constructed ten special versions of the R37, using them to experiment with not only improvements to the chassis, but also various engine modifications, including an innovation for the time, alloy cylinder heads. Its last major success came in the 1926 German GP, ridden by Paul Koppen.

During the late 1920s and early 1930s, BMW concentrated its efforts in the record-breaking field, Ernst Henne waving the company's flag to considerable effect. Riding a 725 cc flat-twin against the stopwatch, Henne assembled an impressive series of speed records at venues which included the heavily-

Georg (Schorsch) Meier pictured in 1948. Just prior to, and immediately after, the war, he was Germany's leading rider. To many, he is still regarded as 'Mr BMW'

banked Avus circuit in Berlin and Germany's first autobahn at Ingolstadt near Munich. Among these feats was the world's fastest for a motorcycle at 137.58 mph.

This set a pattern for another run of outstanding performances by BMW, next demonstrated by Henne in 1932 when he retook the record which had been lost to Britain's Joe Wright and his Zenith-JAP. Wright had achieved a speed of 151.77 mph earlier that year at Tat, Hungary. Henne subsequently raised the record to 152.81 mph at Gyon, also in Hungary.

Henne broke his record yet again in 1935. This time, the venue was a recently-completed section of autobahn just outside Frankfurt, where an average speed of 159.01 mph was recorded. The following year, he was back at the same location once more, but this time with a new, supercharged 495 cc engine. Also new was an all-enclosing, streamlined shell for the machine and rider, which featured a prominent tail fin. This time, Henne raised the record to 168.92 mph.

Some six months later, lone Englishman Eric Fernihough shattered BMW's record on his home-brewed 996 cc JAP V-twin. However, it was only a short while before it fell again, this time to Italy's Piero Taruffi's supercharged, watercooled Gilera four. Within five weeks of the Italian factory's

For 1951 the basically pre-war supercharged Kompressor BMW engine was converted to normally-aspirated form

The 1951 works BMW flat-twin, which had German-made Amal carburettors

BMW works riders, Georg Meier (1) and Walter Zeller (21), during a German championship meeting in May 1951

triumph, at the end of November 1937, Henne put BMW back in the record books. This time, he hoisted the world record to 173.57 mph, where it stayed for some 14 years until it was finally broken by rival NSU (see Chapter 12).

Much of the success garnered by the pairing of Henne and BMW had been possible thanks to supercharging. This had been developed since 1929 when a production R63 had been fitted with a positive-displacement blower that was mounted on the top of the gearbox and driven by the magneto shaft. Lessons gained from this were not only applied to record breaking, but also to the BMW Kompressor 500 works racer, which bore a close resemblance to Henne's machine in technical detail.

Both machines were equipped with a Zoller blower built on to the front of the crankcase assembly and coupled to the rearward-facing inlets by long pipes passing over the cylinders. The cubic capacity was 492 cc (66 × 72 mm), and the dohc (previous engines had been sohc) twin generated

over 80 bhp at 8000 rpm. This gave the bike a maximum road speed of around 140 mph – highly impressive for its era.

The first examples of this new racer made their début in 1935. They employed telescopic front forks at a time when none of the other works racing teams used them. However, it was not until the end of the following year that the first use was made by BMW of plunger rear suspension. When the latter came, its combined use with the teles did not automatically provide the Munich factory with a sufficiently competitive edge, nor did it even equal the other machines, notably the normally-aspirated British singles.

It was not until 1937 that BMW had finally come up with machines which could seriously challenge for honours. That year, the veteran Karl Gall became National Road Racing Champion, while on the Isle of Man, Jock West claimed sixth in the Senior TT. The same rider clinched victory a few weeks later in the Ulster GP to provide BMW with considerable foreign publicity – it was the first time a German machine had won the event.

There were great hopes for 1938, but not only was Gall injured during practice for the Tourist Trophy,

Georg Meier (destined to become European Champion that year) was also forced to retire on the start line. This left West, but although he rode the flat-twin to the limit, he finished no higher than fifth.

It was Georg Meier who made history the following year. He became the first foreign rider to win the IoM Senior TT, then the most important event in the motorcycling sporting calendar.

Meier's team-mate, Jock West, came home second. Unfortunately, this great triumph was tinged with sadness following the death in practice of the third team member, Karl Gall.

A few short weeks later the roar of the racing world was silenced by the outbreak of war. Like the majority of other manufacturers, BMW transferred its industrial might to the military effort.

However, at least BMW was one of the first manufacturers whose machines were raced in the defeated Germany during the immediate post-war days. Various examples of the pre-war flat-twins, including the legendary Kompressor, were campaigned with considerable success.

Furthermore, Georg Meier, who had spent the war in the army, was back in action at the ripe old age of 36. In 1946, Meier formed the Veritas team and selected a BMW (of course!) for his attempt to win the German road-racing championship. By 1949, the

Zeller extracts every last ounce of performance from his BMW at the Solitude circuit, summer 1952

year he was voted Sportsman of the Year in Germany, Meier was back in top form with a string of victories.

The year 1950 saw a battle of the titans between the supercharged giants of BMW and NSU, the latter normally coming out on top.

When Germany was re-admitted to the FIM in 1951, BMW, together with other German manufacturers, had to abandon supercharging. This move favoured the Munich factory much more than NSU, with the result that BMW turned the tables upon its chief domestic rival.

This was amply demonstrated when a remodelled flat-twin made its début in April 1951 at the Eilenriede Rennen races near Hanover. Unlike the new NSU four-cylinder model, the BMW not only lasted the distance, but took the victor's spoils. There was a new rider, too, in the shape of 23-year-old Walter Zeller, who took the chequered flag from team-mate Georg Meier.

However, although top dog in the Fatherland, BMW was not yet ready to dispute the World Championship series. The problem was that against foreign opposition, such as the Italian fours and British singles, the BMW simply was not competitive. This was because the revamped machine, called the Mustang, was little changed from the 1939 Senior TT winner, except that the supercharger had been replaced by conventional air feed and two carburettors.

The new Rennsport appeared in time for the 1953 season. This is Zeller's factory mount for the Isle of Man Senior TT that year. He was an early faller in the race

The following year, 1952, was hardly any better, and it was not until 1953, when Walter Zeller débuted what was to emerge as the Rennsport, was any real improvement made. The German Grand Prix that year was staged over the controversial Schotten circuit. This ten-mile, tree-lined venue was branded as too dangerous by the leading foreign works teams, so the local factories had the field to themselves in the 500 cc race. This resulted in an easy win for Walter Zeller, who rode a modified BMW in which fuel was injected directly into the cylinders instead of the inlet venturis, as on earlier models. At the time, this was said to provide a considerable increase in power, which might have explained Zeller's 35-second lead over team-mate Hans Baltisburger on a conventional 'carburettor' model after only two laps. Another works BMW, ridden by Hans Meier (younger brother of the famous Georg), came home fourth. The FIM later withdrew the points won at Schotten in the 350 and 500 cc classes, however, due to the mass withdrawal of the leading teams.

Zeller had also ridden another of the fuel-injected models in the IoM Senior TT that June. Unfortunately, after lying ninth on the first lap, he spilled early in the race, putting the machine out of action.

In fact, there were three stages in the development of the BMW fuel-injection system. At first, the injector nozzle was fitted between the throttle slide and inlet port, spraying into the induction tract at an angle. Next came the layout employed for Zeller's 1953 Senior TT machine in which the injector was situated in the induction bellmouth, upstream of the throttles and injecting axially. Finally, as first used in the 1953 German GP at Schotten, the nozzle was transferred to the cylinder head, opposite the spark plug. Removal of obstructions from the inlet system improved the cylinder charging appreciably and, thus, resulted in an improved power output figure.

The definitive Rennsport appeared in 1954, and all subsequent factory and 'private' machines were developments of this basic layout.

Originally, the Rennsport engine was a long-stroke unit with 66×72 mm bore and stroke measurements, giving a capacity of 492 cc. In this form, maximum power was produced at 8000 rpm. Later, however, with the need for more power, the bore and stroke measurements were altered to be square at 68×68 mm (493.9 cc), resulting in the engine revolutions rising to 9500 rpm.

The crankshaft, with its 180-degree throws, was of built-up construction. Mainshafts were hollow and integral with their flywheels, which embodied balance weights. Each crankpin hole in the elliptical medial web of the shaft had a shallow counterbore on the side of the web, adjacent to the respective big-end. The radius of the counterbore was greater than that of the end of the web and of the big-end eye so that the shaft's overall length could be kept to the bare minimum.

Like the mainshafts, the hollow crankpins were of 35 mm diameter; one end of each was pressed into the medial web and locked in position by a solid, forced-in expander plug. After the big-end bearings and connecting rods had been assembled on the pins, the cheeks were pressed on and further expander plugs driven in. The plugs at the outer ends of the pins differed from the inner type by having a small longitudinal hole for big-end lubrication.

There were three crankshaft main bearings. The one at the rear was of the self-aligning variety, embodying a special type of roller, while the one at the front was a conventional ball-race type. Another conventional ball-race bearing was housed in the front cover as an outboard support for the timing pinion.

The crankcase was a one-piece Electron casting. There were two 35 mm main bearings which were fitted in separate housings. These housings were

Zeller's 1953 TT engine, showing inlet-manifold fuel-injection delivery pipe and throttle slide

Walter Zeller taking the flag to win the controversial 500 cc German GP, Schotten, 19 July 1953

manufactured from different materials – cast-iron at the front, steel at the rear.

Integral with the forward main bearing housing was the rear wall of the oil pump; the aluminium-alloy pump body carrying the gears was fitted into a recess in the housing to which it was bolted.

The pump itself was of the duplex-gear type, one part feeding the main big-end, while the other supplied the cam gear. Wet-sump lubrication was employed, a 2.8-litre-capacity sump (again in Electron) being bolted to the base of the crankcase.

Oil for the cam gear flowed from the pump, through a series of oilways in the crankcase, to external pipes which lay between the cylinders. These pipes were flanked by a larger-diameter pipe through which the oil returned to the sump.

Lubricant from the other pump circulated from

BMW entered this fully-streamlined model for the Italian GP at Monza in September 1953. The rider was their number-one runner, Walter Zeller

each main bearing housing into a trap secured by screws to the adjacent face of each crankshaft cheek. The trap was essentially a disc which had its periphery turned inwards through 180 degrees to form an annular channel. Oil from the bearing housing was directed by centrifugal force into the channel; it reached the big-end through a small hole in the trap wall that aligned with the aforementioned hole in the crankpin plug. Each of the crankpins had two radial holes and, since they diverged outwards, the oil flow had the maximum centrifugal assistance.

This type of layout minimized internal oilways which otherwise could have weakened the whole crankshaft assembly. In addition, it simplified building up the shaft because no holes had to be aligned.

Left
In 1954 the Munich factory constructed a small number of Rennsport racers for sale to private customers. Unlike the works entries, these employed conventional carburettors

Right
Hans Bartl in action with his Rennsport during 1955. He achieved some excellent placings that year in German national events

Above
Front-end details of Bartl's machine. Note the 2LS front brake, Earles forks and alloy fairing

Below
Walter Zeller awaiting the start. In the mid 1950s his skill was unmatched by any other BMW rider

Finally, the traps acted as very efficient centrifugal filters for collecting sludge and the like, which is why only a gauze suction oil filter system was needed.

Each big-end bearing comprised 14 rollers measuring 10×7 mm. Housed in a duralumin cage, these ran directly on the crankpin and the con-rod eye, both pin and eye featuring specially hardened surfaces.

The connecting rods themselves were of particular interest, as they employed a very unusual flat section, rather than an I-section between the big- and small-ends. Each rod was quite short – about 180

per cent of the stroke. BMW engineers tried the far more conventional I-section type, but discovered that these were far more prone to breakages, fatigue cracks developing at the radius between the flange and web.

The gear case at the front of the engine contained three pairs of spur gears. A steel gear on the crank drove an alloy half-speed gear immediately above it; the gears were lubricated by jet from the front main bearing housing. Also on the crankshaft was a steel gear that meshed with the alloy oil pump driving gear. It was found necessary to embody a cush-drive in the steel gear to prevent the teeth of the alloy gear

from breaking under the load produced by full-throttle acceleration or deceleration of the crankshaft.

A steel gear on the half-speed shaft meshed with the alloy magneto gear which featured slotted holes for timing adjustment. In front of the half-speed gear, and driven from it by a pair of pegs, was a ported sleeve which ran in the Electron front cover and served as a timed engine breather.

Zeller (53) leads Bill Lomas (Guzzi single) during the 1956 500 cc Ulster Grand Prix

Walter Zeller receives a helping hand to push his works BMW to the weigh-in before the 1956 Senior TT. In the race he finished fourth

The breather sleeve contained the coupling for the fuel-injection pump drive. This coupling had holes that engaged with three pegs projecting from the end of the half-speed shaft, and it was splined internally at its forward end to receive male splines on the pump-unit shaft.

At the rear end of the half-speed shaft, which was carried in a pair of ball bearings in a duralumin housing, was a bevel gear. This meshed with two more bevel gears embodying short, hollow shafts which transmitted the drive, via solid shafts, to the camshafts.

Engaging with the splines of the hollow shafts were male splines at the inboard end of the solid drive shafts. Each of these shafts had an integral bevel gear at its outer end and ran in a ball bearing pressed into the inboard half of a cast-iron housing. Split longitudinally in the vertical plane, the housing was held to the cylinder head by three pairs of studs; the two outer pairs also served to retain the Electron cambox covers.

BMW engineers employed a most unconventional arrangement for the double-overhead-camshaft system. In each cylinder head, the two camshafts lay close together within a split housing, and each operated its respective valve through a short, straight rocker. The design was a compromise between the usual sohc and the conventional 'double-knocker' layouts because, although the reciprocating weight with the rockers was higher than with directly-operated valves, there was less power loss since two spur gears replaced the normal five. No doubt, this helped the Rennsport engine to run safely at over 9500 rpm.

Camshafts and rockers ran on needle rollers, while the rocker spindles were carried in the cam housings and had eccentric ends for valve-clearance adjustment.

Typical of the engineering skills shown in its design, the method of locking the rocker spindles was both simple and ingenious. On one end of each spindle was a serrated washer which was located on the spindle by flats. The serrations engaged similar serrations on a short arm, the other end of which was bolted to the housing. If the bolt was slackened and the serrations were disengaged, the spindle could be turned by one serration, or more, and then the serrations re-engaged. For valve timing, there was a vernier coupling between each camshaft and its driving gear.

Each cylinder head contained a part-spherical combustion chamber that provided quite a wide valve included angle of 82 degrees. Inlet and exhaust valve seats were in different materials: manganese steel for the inlet, bronze for the exhaust. Both valve guides were also of bronze.

Valve diameters were 40 mm inlet, and 36 mm exhaust, the latter being sodium-cooled. Duplex coil valve springs and a stepped form of split collet were employed to keep cylinder head width to a minimum.

The downdraught angle of the inlet ports was 15 degrees, and their bore at the flange 32 mm. On the 1954 works-type Rennsport engine, as used by BMW team members that year, the third type of fuel-injection system (already described) was employed. Like the fuel pump, magneto and spark plugs, the injector nozzles were of Bosch manufacture and had a minimum delivery pressure of 570 psi.

Fuel was gravity-fed from the 25-litre tank to a paper cartridge filter mounted on the offside of the crankcase, above the cylinder. From the filter, petrol passed to the pump, which was of the plunger type (similar to pumps used on diesel engines). There was no direct rider control of pump delivery.

In the pump body was a diaphragm, which was

*A year later and Zeller in action on a streamlined
BMW during the 1957 Senior. The picture was taken
at the Bungalow. After holding third place at the end
of lap 1, he was destined to retire while still in the
same position on lap 4*

subjected on one side to induction-pipe depression
by means of a balance-pipe system connected to the
two throttle boxes. Attached to the diaphragm was a
rack-rod, which engaged with a gear on each of the
two plungers. Movement of the diaphragm, acti-
vated by opening or closing the throttle, rotated the
plungers; such rotation varied the internal porting
and, with it, the amount of fuel delivered by the
plungers. Surplus fuel was pumped back into the
tank. An adjusting screw permitted basic setting of
the mixture strength. Lubrication of the pump was
taken care of by engine oil from a separate $\frac{1}{2}$-litre
container.

Apart from providing a useful gain in performance, BMW also claimed, at the time, that its fuel-
injection system produced a 15-per-cent improvement in fuel consumption.

Another aspect of the Rennsport engine, which
was of considerable technical interest, was the piston
design. Almost fully-skirted, the 10.2:1 pistons had
an oil scraper ring below the bosses of the gudgeon

pin. Three compression rings were also fitted in the
conventional position, the lowest of these having a
tapered face and drainage holes to assist oil control.

The piston crown was of nearly pent-roof shape
and fitted closely into the head space at each side to
promote squish. To accommodate the contour of the
valve head, the valve cutaways under the inlet and
exhaust valves were convex and concave
respectively.

The cylinder barrels normally featured shrunk-in
cast-iron liners, but BMW also tried chromium-
plated bores – the finish being applied directly to the
aluminium – with complete success.

A taper at the rear of the crankshaft accommo-
dated a flywheel car-type clutch. The clutch body
was in two halves, which were held together by a
ring of eight bolts; the inner face of the rear half
formed one of the driving surfaces. Sandwiched
between that face and the pressure plate was a single,
faced driven plate. This had a splined centre which
transmitted the drive to the gearbox mainshaft.

The rear half of the clutch body had internal
peripheral teeth which engaged with similar external teeth on the pressure plate. Actuating force for
the pressure plate was supplied by six non-
adjustable springs that were seated in the front half
of the clutch body. Clutch withdrawal was by means

Following Zeller's retirement at the end of 1957, BMW signed up the former Norton and Gilera World Champion, Geoff Duke, for the 1958 season

of a thrust rod passing through the hollow gearbox mainshaft; a hemispherical pad, jointed to the end of the rod, sat on a cup in the centre of the pressure plate.

The forward half of the clutch body had a spigot that fitted into a bore in the back of the rear main bearing housing. There was an oil seal within this bore, and the spigot had a spiral groove to assist in preventing oil from entering the clutch housing. Clutch cooling was effected by a series of concentric ribs on the rear of the clutch body, and by air ducts in the housing.

Of conventional, all-indirect design, the gearbox had a top gear reduction of 1.3:1 and normally had five ratios (although four were used for certain circuits).

The complete engine/gearbox assembly was supported at three points in the frame: one each at front and rear of the lower portion of the crankcase, and the third at a steady point above cylinder level in the crankcase half of the gear case. The frame was of the cradle type with a tubular extension to carry the racing seat and to provide anchorages for the rear suspension legs. On the works bikes, three different frame layouts were evolved to ensure that each rider could tuck himself away to the maximum advantage.

Pivoted-fork rear suspension, first seen on works BMWs in 1952, was employed, a feature being the enclosure of the drive shaft within the offside fork tube. Likewise, an Earles-type front fork first appeared for the 1953 season, replacing the telescopic

Above right
Duke pictured during the 1958 Senior TT from which he retired with brake trouble. His period with BMW was generally disappointing and he soon reverted to a privately-entered Norton

Right
The 1958 German 500 cc National Champion, Ernst Hiller. He is seen here competing in the Senior event at Thruxton that year

fork which BMW had done so much to popularize. Front and rear suspension legs were similar in design and embodied two-way hydraulic damping; variations in road conditions or riders' weights could easily be met by fitting legs with the appropriate spring and damper characteristics.

Both brakes were cable-operated, the front one being of the two-leading-shoe pattern. BMW stated that the new fork improved front wheel braking by eliminating 'dip' when the brake was applied.

The 1954-specification works Rennsport produced significant power from around 6500 rpm, with a maximum output of 58 bhp at 8500 rpm using

Left
Besides Geoff Duke, another British rider who rode for BMW during the late 1950s was Dickie Dale. Like Duke, eventually he also switched to a Norton single

Below
During the 1970s, tyre tester Helmut Dahne put up some remarkable performances, notably in the Isle of Man, on a race-kitted, pushrod-roadster-based BMW. Dahne is shown here in the 1974 event

injectors, and 52 bhp with conventional carburettors.

Besides the factory machines, a batch of 25 Rennsports was manufactured in 1954 for sale to private customers. These engines, together with the factory units, were not only to be used in solo racing BMWs but, as the next chapter will reveal, also to achieve unparalleled success in the sidecar class.

On the solo front, 1956 was to be the Munich factory's premier year. This witnessed Walter Zeller finish a superb second in the World Championship series to John Surtees and MV Agusta. When one considers that Zeller finished in front of the entire Gilera team, among others, it was a notable achievement, even though his best placings were a couple of seconds – at Assen and Spa – and the season was upset by the riders' strike that took place at the Dutch TT. This hit several of the leading riders, including Geoff Duke.

By then, Zeller was using a very special shortstroke engine, with 70 × 64 mm dimensions, giving well over 60 bhp. There were several other differences compared to the Rennsport engine, notably the drive shaft, which ran alongside the fork leg, not inside it. Full streamlining was a feature of the machine, although this was not employed when Zeller finished fourth in the 1956 Senior TT.

A little-known fact is that BMW also built a prototype 250-class racer. Coded RS250, this was constructed in 1954 for Zeller to challenge Haas and NSU. With bore and stroke dimensions of 56 × 50.6 mm, the RS was essentially a miniature version of its larger dohc, flat-twin brother. However, development was halted after a few hours' testing due to financial constraints, caused by poor sales of the company's production roadsters.

At the end of the 1957 season, there were two important developments which affected BMW's solo racing effort – the FIM ban on full streamlining and Walter Zeller's retirement from the sport.

For the following season, Geoff Duke and Dickie Dale both rode factory-supported models (Duke's was said to have been Zeller's actual bike), but neither of these established stars could match the success gained by Zeller. Although several German riders, among them Ernst Hiller put up some good performances, and Dale continued to ride for BMW in 1959, followed by the dashing Japanese rider Fumio Ito in 1960, the German flat-twin's effectiveness as a competitive solo racer was over. What little money there was at that time went to supporting the much more successful sidecar boys.

3
BMW sidecars

Phenomenal is the only word for the overwhelming success of the double-overhead-camshaft, BMW flat-twin engine in the Sidecar World Championship during the two decades from the mid 1950s to the mid 1970s. In the 21 years from 1954 until 1974 inclusive, BMW-engined outfits took the title on 19 occasions!

As recorded in the previous chapter, except for the immediate pre-war period, when the Munich factory's supercharged machinery ruled supreme, the German flat-twins had not been particularly successful. However, having once realized this, BMW switched much of its effort into the sidecar class where its subsequent dominance emphasized the engine's greater suitability for the three-wheel sector of the sport.

In sidecar racing, the engine's width was no disadvantage, nor, for that matter, was its shaft drive, while its silky smoothness and great engine torque were a positive boon. The engine could be slung ultra-low for faster cornering, while the cylinders were cooled effectively. Another great advantage was the high standard of engineering quality and its resultant reliability. The 180-degree crankshaft was extraordinarily robust, as were its other major components.

Wilhelm Noll and passenger Fritz Cron won BMW's first Sidecar World Championship and, thus, laid the foundation for an unparalleled run of success in this branch of the sport

Until 1954, the world of sidecar racing had been dominated by the British driver Eric Oliver, who raced a series of outfits powered by the venerable single-cylinder Norton engine. During this period, the highest BMW-powered sidecars had finished in classic races since the instigation of the new World Championship in 1949, were the third positions gained by Kraus and Huser in the 1953 Belgian GP, and Noll and Cron in the Swiss GP the same year.

Oliver had started his championship defence in his usual winning style, taking the first three rounds of the 1954 series in the Isle of Man, Ulster and Belgium.

The next round was scheduled to be staged on BMW's home ground at the Solitude circuit, near Stuttgart. However, a week prior to this, both Oliver and his passenger, Leslie Nutt, were injured when their outfit skidded off a wet track at a non-championship meeting near Frankfurt in mid July. In the accident, Oliver broke his arm, while Nutt injured a shoulder. Without the four-times World Champion, the German Grand Prix was a walk-over for the pair of factory BMW outfits driven by Noll and Cron and Schneider and Strauss.

Although Oliver bravely rode in the next round in Switzerland, Wilhelm Noll and Fritz Cron put an end to the English supremacy, taking the title with three straight victories (Germany, Switzerland and Italy) – as many wins as the Oliver/Nutt combination, but

Above
Noll employed this early form of streamlining on his BMW outfit at the Belgian Grand Prix in July 1954

Below
A couple of months later, Noll's machine had this comprehensive streamlined alloy shell when he raced to victory at Monza on 12 September

their superior finishing positions in the other three races made all the difference.

BMW finished the year with not only Noll and Cron as champions, but Schneider and Strauss fourth, with Hillebrand and Grünwald fifth in the title chase.

In 1955, the title went to Willi Faust and Karl Remmert, who won three of the six rounds in Spain, Germany and Holland. However, the pair crashed their works BMW outfit during a practice session at Hockenheim later in the season, and the brilliant

The unstreamlined works BMW of Willi Faust, Isle of Man TT, 1955

partnership was broken by the death of Remmert. Faust recovered after a long period in hospital, but never raced again.

On 4 October 1955, Wilhelm Noll broke a total of 18 sidecar world records when he rode a specially prepared, fuel-injected flat-twin fitted with a streamlined shell that featured an enclosed cabin and a rear stabilizing fin. The sidecar wheel was also streamlined. The records broken included: flying kilometre at 174 mph; mile, 174 mph; five kilometres, 168.5 mph; and five miles at 165.5 mph; standing-start kilometre, 86.5 mph; and mile at 103 mph.

Noll's efforts had recaptured the world's fastest three-wheel record for Germany, his speed of 174 mph being some 12 mph quicker than the previous record held by Bob Burns with a 998 cc Vincent V-twin. He then went on to cap an outstanding personal effort by winning a second world title to add to the one he had won in 1954. In 1956, he and passenger Fritz Cron became World Sidecar Champions once more. They won in Belgium, Germany and Ulster, and finished second in Holland.

Left
BMW hydraulic rear brake as used on the factory outfits during the mid 1950s

After this, Noll announced his retirement. In 1957, he tried his hand at car racing, but without success.

Next in the line of world sidecar champions came the former Luftwaffe pilot, Fritz Hillebrand, and his passenger, Manfred Grünwald. After dominating the 1957 title series with wins in the first three rounds (Germany, Isle of Man and Holland) and a third position in Belgium, the team suffered a terminal blow when they were involved in a serious accident after becoming champions.

At an international meeting in Bilbao, on 24 August 1957, their outfit crashed, killing Fritz Hillebrand. Manfred Grünwald sustained only minor hand injuries, but decided to retire.

After a drastic fall-off in sales of its production models, BMW only supported one sidecar crew for the 1958 season. This was the pairing of Walter Schneider and Hans Strauss, who had finished as runners-up in the previous year to Hillebrand and Grünwald.

However, if the works pair thought that they were in for a walk-over, they could not have been more mistaken. The privateers Florian Camathias and Hilmar Cecco, on a home-tuned Rennsport outfit, gave them a fight in every one of the four rounds of the title series. In fact, the Swiss pair (who both raced solos as well) won the Dutch TT at Assen.

Another serious contender for honours that year was Helmut Fath, who displayed his future potential for the first time to a wider audience.

Schneider and Strauss retained their title in 1959 when, once more, their biggest challenge came from

Overleaf
The 1957 Sidecar World Champion, Fritz Hillebrand, and Manfred Grünwald on their way to victory in the IoM TT. Their average speed was a record 71.89 mph

Below
World Champion Wilhelm Noll with BMW press officer Carl Hoepner. The occasion was when Noll broke a series of speed records in October 1955 on a section of the Munich-Ingolstadt autobahn

Privateers A. Ritter and E. Blaunth pilot their BMW outfit during the 1958 TT

Camathias and Cecco, whom they beat by a mere four points. In the five-round series, the Germans won three races, the Swiss the remaining two.

Schneider and Strauss decided to call it a day and retire after winning their second title. Like Noll, Schneider tried his hand at motor racing, but also without success.

Many expected Camathias and Cecco to become the next champions. However, things did not pan out that way, for Cecco split with Camathias and joined his rival, Edgar Strub.

With a new passenger, Camathias had a poor season, his best placing being a second at Solitude in the final round. He finished the season down in fourth place in the final ratings. So who finished in front of him? The answer is Fath, Fritz Scheidegger and the Englishman Pip Harris.

Winners of four of the five Grands Prix contested in 1960, Helmut Fath and Alfred Wohlgemuth dominated the three-wheel category that year. However, as recounted in Chapter 5, a serious accident at the Nürburgring in 1961 halted a very promising career. Wohlgemuth was killed and Fath spent many months in hospital. He eventually returned with his own four-cylinder engine in 1966 – after BMW had refused to provide backing for a comeback.

Not only had Fath been sidelined, but Camathias had been too. Intent on a serious crack at the world crown in 1961, the diminutive Swiss star had joined with his old 'ballast', Hilmar Cecco, and much was

expected of them. However, at a meeting at Modena, Italy, in mid May, Cecco sustained fatal injuries when the pair crashed their BMW. Camathias was also badly injured – to the extent that he did not race for the remainder of that season.

This tragic turn of events threw the championship wide open. The factory-supported pairing of Max Deubel and Emil Horner became champions, while the privateers Scheidegger and Burckart were runners-up.

If luck had favoured them in 1961, it was skill and determination alone that brought Deubel and Horner their second title in 1962. They gave their challengers, Camathias and Scheidegger, little chance of glory. These three teams dominated the series, except in the Isle of Man where all three retired, leaving victory to a grateful Chris Vincent and Eric Bliss with a specially-prepared, twin-cylinder, pushrod, BSA roadster-engined outfit.

For the next two years (1963 and 1964), Deubel and Horner retained their championship laurels, their only real challenge being the outfits of Scheidegger and Camathias. However, this run of success came to an end during 1965 and 1966 when the Deubel/Horner partnership was unseated by the newly-formed pairing of Scheidegger and Robinson. They then retired from the sport at the end of 1966, Deubel to run his hotel in Muhlenau, and Horner returning to his former occupation of car mechanic.

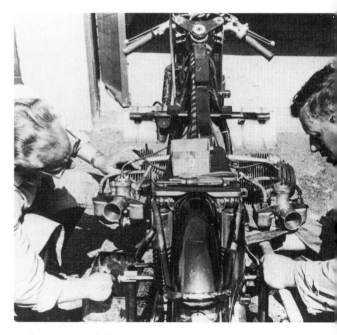

TT practice, 1959. Schneider's BMW with works mechanics. Note the massive Dell'Orto carbs and swish bowls

Above

Helmut Fath and passenger Alfred Wohlgemuth totally dominated the 1960 World Championship series. The following year they looked set to repeat this performance, but a horrific accident at the Nürburgring left Wohlgemuth dead and Fath badly injured

Below

Max Deubel took up the BMW mantle after Fath's accident, winning the title in the four years from 1961 to 1964. Deubel is shown here with his chair-man, Horner, during the 1962 TT – they retired on the last lap having had victory within their grasp

Fritz Scheidegger grass-tracking with his BMW road-racing outfit, Switzerland, 1962

Scheidegger, together with his fellow Swiss Camathias, had brought to an end the long supremacy of German sidecar drivers.

Once again, however, fate was to strike at the very top of the sidecar world, as first Camathias (Brands Hatch, 10 October 1965) and then Scheidegger (Mallory Park, 26 March 1967) were involved in fatal accidents. Both were caused through mechanical failure, rather than rider error.

The deaths of the two Swiss stars, and Deubel's retirement, benefited the up-and-coming partnership of Klaus Enders and Ralf Engelhardt. They won five of the eight events to lift the 1967 championship crown.

In 1968, Helmut Fath stunned the racing world by becoming the first man to win a world championship with a machine he had built himself. However, with Fath striking mechanical problems, Enders and Engelhardt, with BMW backing, won their second title in 1969.

With a new passenger, Wolfgang Kallaugh, Klaus Enders took his third championship in 1970. At the end of the year, he decided to retire, at 33, moving to four wheels. This let in Horst Owesle and Peter Rutherford who (as recounted in Chapter 10) took

the title for the Münch team in 1971.

For 1972, three-times champion Klaus Enders arrived back on the scene. His four-wheel career – still with BMW – had not achieved the level of success to which he was accustomed. Consequently, he decided to don his leathers once more and re-enter the sidecar-racing arena.

Passengered by his old chum, Ralf Engelhardt, Enders proved that he had made the right decision

Camathias' BMW 'kneeler' outfit, 1964

Scheidegger and English passenger John Robinson, 1964 Dutch TT at Assen

Below
Florian Camathias (left) after winning the sidecar event at Scarborough's international, 19 September 1959. On the right is a youthful Mike Hailwood

by winning his fourth sidecar crown. This put him on level pegging with those other two great three-wheel legends, Eric Oliver and Max Deubel.

This success spurred Enders to even greater effort. In 1973, he not only became the first man on three wheels to win five world titles, but he won all of the seven rounds that he contested!

It was perhaps fitting that Enders should be the man to win BMW's last sidecar championship in 1974, and so create a record which still stands. However, this final year was not the relatively easy series of victories to which he had become accustomed. Instead, there were problems with his new Büsch-tuned engine, as well as the ever-increasing competition from the two-strokes, headed by König.

Enders decided to retire (for real this time) rather than race a two-stroke, having scored a record total of 27 GP victories – all on BMWs. Strangely, after that final championship year, no BMW-powered sidecar ever won another Grand Prix!

During the 21 seasons in which the BMW had been a serious contender for sidecar championship honours, the power output of the dohc, flat-twin engine had not altered, as lap times may have

A scene at Brands Hatch at the end of the 1966 season. Left to right: Fritz Scheidegger, Max Deubel, John Robinson and Emil Horner

suggested. The engine remained almost the same as it had been in the mid 1950s. It was the chassis to which the engineers had turned their attention in an effort to raise the performance.

From 1958, a major change had been introduced to the works BMW outfits (pioneered by Eric Oliver's Norton back in 1954). This saw the riding position transferred from the conventional sitting to a kneeling stance. The resultant lowering of gravity provided much improved cornering abilities. The fuel tank was also moved. At first, it was split into two and lowered; later, it was joined again and housed in the sidecar.

Another development was the replacement of the telescopic front forks by a type of suspension that was more akin to that of a car than a motorcycle. In many ways, the same could be said about the wheels, brakes and tyres.

Streamlining was another aspect that played a vital role in the development of the modern racing sidecar outfit. The 'chairs' had not been affected by the revised FIM regulation which had banned full streamlining from solos after the end of the 1957 season.

Towards the end of its reign as World Sidecar Champion, the BMW factory itself ceased direct support. Its place was taken by several entrants, notably men such as Büsch and Krauser – the latter would later win world-wide fame through his motorcycle luggage empire.

Thus, the curtain was drawn on a truly illustrious era, which saw BMW engines employed by all the leading sidecar exploiters of the day. They achieved a record number of championship titles in this branch of motorcycle sport which has yet to be equalled.

West German GP, May 1967. BMW outfits of Klaus Enders (18) followed by Georg Auerbacher, Pip Harris, Siegfried Schauzu, Tony Wakefield and Colin Seeley

4
DKW – *das kleine wünder*

Together with BMW and NSU, DKW ranks as one of the major German companies that pioneered the motorcycle up to World War 2. Thereafter, it thrust its development to new horizons in the years now known as the 'classic' period.

The history of the DKW marque began with the birth of its founder, Jorgen Skafte Rasmussen, on 30 July 1878 in Nakskow, Denmark. The young Rasmussen moved to Düsseldorf, Germany, in 1904 and then, in 1907, to Zschopau, 20 kilometres south of Chemnitz in Saxony (today called Karl Marx Stadt). Here, he was involved in several engineering ventures with a partner called Ernst, manufacturing and selling machines and tools ranging from boiler fittings to fire lighters and domestic appliances.

In 1916, inspired by the acute wartime fuel shortages, Rasmussen began to experiment with a steam car, the *Dampf Kraft Wagen*. Even though this was not proceeded with, it provided the first use of the now-famous DKW initials.

The next event of significance came in 1919 when Rasmussen produced an 18 cc toy two-stroke engine (designed by Hugo Ruppe). This was known as *Das Knaben Wünsch* (the schoolboy's dream), and it led to engine production, the company's first full year in this sector of engineering being taken up largely with development and research. The first fruits of this effort came the following year, 1921, with the début of the Ruppe-designed 122 cc auxiliary engine. This sold extremely well (some 25,000 units had been sold by mid 1922).

Next came motorized bicycles, 'armchair' motorcycles (forerunners of the modern motor scooter), and finally full-blown conventional motorcycles. By 1926, DKW had manufactured its 100,000th engine assembly, while the motorcycle range included machines with capacities of 200, 250, 350 and 500 cc.

From then on, things simply took off, with a vast empire growing at ever-increasing speed. For example, in 1928, DKW took over Audi and produced the first DKW car, the Type 15. Three years later, with a workforce of over 20,000, it could claim

Ewald Kluge and Siegfried Wünsche rebuilding one of the pre-war works supercharged DKW 250s, circa 1950

to be the largest motorcycle manufacturer in the world. However, all this growth had created side-effects – the most significant being high losses and massive bank debts, as much of the expansion had come just prior to the start of the Depression. However, Rasmussen was able to bail out his tottering organization by way of an innovative merger which saw Audi, DKW, Horch and Wanderer join forces to form Auto Union AG in 1932. This new grouping was headed by Dipl. Ing. Carl Hahn and underwritten by the State Bank of Saxony.

Left
Works rider H. P. Müller on the new twin-cylinder DKW, summer 1951

Right
The Wolf-designed 250 DKW twin featured square (54 × 54 mm) bore and stroke dimensions, together with rotary-valve induction. This is the 1952 version

The new combine took as its trademark four interlinked silver circles, which continue today on the up-market Audi car range. The merger coincided with the gradual easing of the financial gloom which had swept the industrialized world during the early 1930s, with the result that it was a huge commercial success. Both its two- and four-wheel products sold well throughout the remainder of the decade up to the outbreak of World War 2 in 1939.

Of the four companies, only DKW made motor-cycles. Besides its bikes, however, the Zschopau company was also very much a trend-setter on four wheels, typified by the hugely successful F-series cars. Over 250,000 of these had been made by the time production was finally halted in November 1942.

The prototype three-cylinder DKW which caused such a sensation when it was first wheeled out at Hockenheim in early May 1952, Unfortunately, its original performance left much to be desired

No four-wheel racing enthusiast worth his salt does not know of the legendary achievements of the Auto Union racing team in the mid-late 1930s. On two wheels, DKW was almost as well known, both in Germany and abroad, during this same period.

As far back as 1925, DKW had entered the racing fray with 175 and 250 cc machinery using, of course, two-strokes, but with intercooling and the Bichrome system of supercharging. However, it was not until 1931, when the Hermann Weber-designed split-single layout appeared, that the marque enjoyed any real success.

'Siggi' Wünsche with the new 350 DKW triple during the Swiss GP at Berne, May 1952

August Prüssing, who worked in the DKW racing department alongside Weber, was also involved with the successful development. During the next few years, just about every one of Germany's top riders raced DKWs at one time or another. Riders such as Fleischmann, Herz, Steinbach, Klein, Müller, Ley, Rosemeyer, Wünsche, Kluge and Winkler all piloted the screaming 'Deeks'.

The first of the new generation of split-singles was a quarter-litre machine in which the supercharging piston operated in front of the crankcase. Models based on this machine went on to achieve a truly amazing haul of victories and lap records through-out, what were for DKW, the golden 1930s. Before long, DKW's track reputation had spread outside the German frontiers, and in their day, those machines were often winning in faster times than the 350s. DKW even ventured to the Isle of Man for the famous TT series – the very heart of the mighty British racing empire.

At the Berlin show in 1935, DKW débuted an 'over-the-counter' racer, the SS250. This was based on the all-conquering works machinery and used the same basic split-single, watercooled power unit.

In 1938, Ewald Kluge (who had initially led the 1937 Lightweight TT) became the first German to win an Isle of Man race when he took his 250 DKW to victory.

The following year, 1939, DKW not only had the largest racing department in the world, with around 150 engineers, but also some extremely competitive machinery. This included the 250 US, a supercharged, double-piston twin that pumped out an impressive 40 bhp at 7000 rpm, and a similar 350 producing 48 bhp. These bikes also had the dubious honour of producing the world's most ear-splitting sound, their exhaust notes drowning every other machine on the circuit!

One example of each engine capacity was also specially prepared for speed record attempts, and running on alcohol fuel, they produced 49 and 60 bhp respectively. These machines were the last for which the brilliant Hermann Weber was responsible (he was destined to die in Russia after the war).

A disappointment came at the 1939 TT where, although DKW fielded an extremely strong team in a bid to dominate the proceedings in both the 250 and 350 cc races, the best it could achieve was a second (Kluge) behind the lone Benelli single of Mellors in the Lightweight.

However, on the Continent that year, the 'Deeks' were dominant, gaining victories in Holland, Sweden and Germany.

Then, in early Sepember, came the outbreak of war, and for six long years competitive motorcycle sport was shelved while an altogether more deadly game was fought out between the Axis powers and the Allies.

If wartime had brought its problems, then peace, when it finally came in May 1945, was traumatic, to say the least, for the DKW marque. Not only had all four of Auto Union's main factories been severely damaged by Allied bombing, but they were also in the Russian sector when Germany was partitioned. (The former DKW plant went on to make motorcycles for the Eastern Bloc countries, first under the name IFA and then MZ – see Chapter 11).

Auto Union elected to move West. For the company's rebirth in the new West Germany, DKW selected Ingolstadt on the River Danube, in Upper Bavaria. Here, the first post-war business conducted was the servicing of ex-military vehicles, rather than the manufacture of any new machinery. However, 1947 saw the formation of Auto Union GmbH which, initially, was engaged in the manufacture of spare parts for pre-war DKW cars and motorcycles. Currency reforms in the summer of the following year allowed some of the pre-war Auto Union management to raise enough capital to relaunch vehicle manufacture. In effect, this move refinanced the Auto Union company.

The first project by the new organization was the introduction of an improved version of the piston-ported RT125 roadster. However, even before this, DKWs had appeared on the race circuit once again.

Crankshaft, cylinders and pistons of the 1953-type 350 DKW

Dipl. Ing. Wolf created the three-cylinder model after getting the idea from originally fitting a magneto at the front of the crankcase on one of the 250 twins

As early as 1947, some of the pre-war works bikes had been given an airing. Remarkably, some had survived the war – in barns and cellars, and in at least one case, actually buried!

Then, in May 1948 at Hockenheim, a racing version of the RT125 appeared. This made quite a respectable showing against the mainly NSU opposition. Later, ridden by Kluge, Wünsche and Müller, it was raced in modified form with rear-facing twin exhaust, high-level megaphones, magneto ignition (the original had battery/coil), nearside-mounted carb, rev-counter, plunger rear suspension, oil-damped telescopic front forks and a larger-diameter, full-width front stopper.

By 1949, both the racing 125 and the pre-war supercharged, double-piston twins were becoming the quickest machinery in German Lightweight racing events. Just how competitive they were was illustrated by the leading racer of the day, the Scot Fergus Anderson. He was also a part-time journalist who, writing in his 'Continental Chatter' column in the 17 November 1949 issue of *Motor Cycling* said: 'Most memorable incident at Cologne: I was doing a little training on my 500 cc Gambalunga (Moto Guzzi) just in case the powers-that-be said ''yes'', and had it wound up to maximum revolutions in the biggest gear – when a machine came creeping inexorably past me in the middle of a long straight. It was Walfried Winkler on the four-piston 250 cc DKW!'

This version of the Wolf-designed 250 DKW twin with rear-facing exhausts appeared during practice for the 1953 Italian Grand Prix

Obviously, one has to take into account that unlike 'foreign' manufacturers, DKW, together with other German marques such as NSU and BMW, was able to use blowers, whereas in other countries supercharging had been banned by the FIM in 1946. None the less, DKW was still top dog in the Fatherland, 'Siggi' Wünsche taking the 350 cc German Championship title.

This state of affairs was not to continue, as not only were DKW's rivals developing new machinery, but in the spring of 1950 came news that Germany was to be re-admitted to the FIM in time for the 1951 season.

DKW, together with the other major producers, responded by announcing that it would be entering the international fray with new normally-aspirated 'strokers' in both the 125 and 250 cc categories. Its team was to comprise Kluge, Müller and Wünsche — all competitors of considerable experience and ability.

At the first meeting of the 1951 road-race season, the Eilenriede-Rennen at Hanover on 29 April, DKW débuted its latest machinery, as did its principal rivals, BMW and NSU. The Ingolstadt company's

offering included an all-new 247.3 cc parallel twin. The cylinders were inclined slightly forward from the vertical, each having its own Dell'Orto carb. The sparking plugs were placed centrally for maximum efficiency, while the ignition was taken care of by a Bosch flywheel magneto. The clutch ran in an oil bath and was mounted on the nearside with chain primary drive. Suspension was taken care of by an oil-damped telescopic front fork and a swinging arm at the rear with twin, hydraulically-damped shocks. The frame was of the all-welded, tubular, full-duplex variety.

Setting off the bike was a massive, hand-beaten, alloy fuel tank. The combined rear mudguard/number plate and the front mudguard were also in the same material. Some machines were fitted with a small fairing, again in alloy.

The designs of the all-new 250 twin and the revamped 125 single were the responsibility of Dipl. Ing. Erich Wolf. He had made his reputation as a private tuner of the earlier DKW engines, together with the Austrian Puch split-single, before joining the Ingolstadt factory. Number two in the DKW design team was another young engineer, Dipl. Ing. Jacob.

Although Wolf increased the power output of the new twin from its initial 20 to 23 bhp, he could not succeed in making it competitive against the top four-stroke 250s of the day, such as the Italian Benelli and Moto Guzzi machines.

In their attempts to extract more power, Wolf and Jacob not only tried numerous induction systems with different discs, pistons, cylinders, heads and the like, but also carried out an extensive weight-pruning exercise. Eventually, the works 250 'Deek' became the lightest machine in its class. Although these changes resulted in a superior power-to-weight ratio, they also led to mechanical and structural unreliability, which proved counter-productive.

Thus, it was not until the following year, 1952, that any real results were seen from the team's work. The 250 parallel twin was significantly improved by the fitment of a Bosch magneto in place of the flywheel magneto, a single Dell'Orto carburettor and, most important of all, a change in the design of the exhaust system. The latter had a pair of expansion chambers in place of the original noisy, but largely ineffective, megaphones. This was one of the earliest, if not the first, motorcycles to be so equipped in Germany, possibly the world. Moreover, as Wolf discovered, this relatively simple move enabled the DKW design to gain a relatively large increase in power output.

German GP, 1955. August Hobl on a DKW (66) leads Norton rider John Surtees during the 350 cc race at the Karussel, Nürburgring

Weird-looking streamlined nose fitted to works DKW triple at the 1954 Dutch TT

The first appearance of the latest DKW twin was at Hockenheim in mid May. The riders now comprised the veterans Kluge and Wünsche, plus two newcomers — Karl Hofmann and Rudi Felgenheier. Müller had left to ride for Horex (and later NSU).

However, the most interesting news of all at Hockenheim was the appearance of a three-cylinder 'Deek'. This had come about purely by chance. In an

attempt to solve ignition problems, Wolf had modified the 250 twins by fitting the magneto (and also
the inlet disc) in front of the crankcase. It was this
that had given him the idea of actually fitting a third
cylinder in place of the magneto at the front of the
crankcase, to create a 350. In this way, one of the
most innovative racing designs of the 1950s was
born.

*Control layout of the 1956-type 125 single. Note chin-
pad, tacho and the battery mounted behind the
windscreen*

*'Little and Large' at the 1955 Italian GP: left, one of
the new 125 single-cylinder models, and right, the
latest 350 triple. Both were the work of Helmut Görg*

Both the 125 single and 250 twin DKWs featured
square 54 × 54 mm bore and stroke measurements,
but for the new three-cylinder model, in order to
restrict the swept volume to 350 cc, the bore of each
cylinder was reduced to 53 mm and the stroke was
fixed at 52.8 mm. This gave each cylinder a capacity
of just over 116 cc – totalling 348.48 cc. The two
outer cylinders were inclined slightly forward at 15
degrees from the vertical to assist the cooling of the
rear of the aircooled cylinders, resulting in an
included cylinder angle of 75 degrees.

To produce the desired 120-degree firing interval
between the cylinders, DKW employed offset crankpins, the central 17.5 mm big-end leading the nearside one by 165 degrees and trailing its offside
partner by 45 degrees. In addition, the Ingolstadt
engineers reverted to piston-port induction, with a
28 mm Dell'Orto SS1 carb for each cylinder (using
their own specially-designed float chambers).

A six-cylinder-type magneto, from a BMW 328
car, was fitted to the offside of the crankcase and
driven at half engine speed by a spur gear off the
crankshaft.

As this 'new' engine was fitted into the rolling
chassis of the 250 twin, on paper, it had an excellent
chance of achieving outstanding power-to-weight

ratio figures. However, the initial power output was a disappointing 31 bhp.

The prototype made its classic début at the 1952 Swiss Grand Prix, but Wünsche was forced out on lap 12 with engine trouble, after holding fifth spot.

The next outing came at the home round, in front of a hugely partisan crowd of 400,000 spectators. Two of the new triples were entered, ridden by Kluge and Wünsche; both created drama at the Solitude circuit near Stuttgart.

On lap 12, Kluge caught up with the leading Nortons at the front of the field, only to fall. With his shoulder blade broken, he retrieved the DKW, remounted and came home in sixth place, but was rushed straight to hospital. Meanwhile, Wünsche had ridden most of the race without his nearside footrest, to finish a hard-earned 11th – a popular result with his many fans in the vast crowd.

In the 125 race, all the DKWs retired, but in the 250 event, Rudi Felgenheier (a last-minute substitute for the injured Kluge) scored the factory's first post-war GP victory.

Generally, however, classic outings that year were severely limited by the time needed to sort the bugs out of the new three-cylinder model, but progress was being made. The most important modification

The definitive version of the three-cylinder model. It was not only faster and more reliable, but, at last, was also on a par with the best Italian bikes

that year came in August with the introduction of a new lubrication system. Right from its first race, the triple had been prone to piston seizures as a result of using a straight petroil mixture. This was supplemented at first, and then replaced entirely by direct lubrication to cylinder walls and main bearings. The oil was carried in the top frame tube and fed by gravity through a multiplicity of small pipes and needle valves.

The Ingolstadt factory announced its team in early 1953, the riders being unchanged (Kluge, Wünsche, Felgenheier and Hofmann), but the 125 had been dropped. Wolf and Jacob had spent much of the winter working on the 250 twin. The problems of the single rotary valve and its single carburettor, which led to unequal inlet tract lengths, were tackled by simply turning the rotary valve through 90 degrees and relocating it between the cylinder barrels so that it ran fore and aft, parallel to the wheelbase. The single carburettor was at one end and the forward-facing magneto at the other. This change, together with more work to the exhaust, increased the power to 22 bhp – enough to help Wünsche and a new works rider, August Hobl, to several leaderboard placings that year in the quarter-litre category. Even so, the Ingolstadt models were not quick enough to match the class-leading Moto Guzzi and NSU four-strokes.

At the Italian GP at Monza, in September, one of the 250 twins sported rearward-facing exhausts and

twin carbs. However, although this was used in practice, it did not make the race.

Meanwhile, the three-cylinder model had received limited improvements to its power unit, aimed at increasing reliability. As before, great effort had been expended upon paring the dry weight of the machines to a bare minimum. This meant that the frame tubing was of the narrowest gauge thought practical, while the brakes were just adequate. So seriously was the weight-saving issue taken that there were four sizes of aluminium-alloy fuel tank (interchangeable between the two engine capacities). These held 12, 22, 28 and 32 litres.

The IoM TT was the first of the 1953 classics. Prior to this, in May, team leader Ewald Kluge had suffered a broken leg when he had crashed at the Nürburgring during a German National Championship event. Many observers believed that this would stop the DKW team from honouring their entries, which had been made before the Kluge accident.

However, the DKW équipe duly arrived in Douglas (but not until half-way through practice

Engine and exhaust details of the 1956 350

week) with Siegfried Wünsche and the substitute for Kluge, Rudi Felgenheier, accompanied by race chief Wolf and a couple of mechanics. They had a major task in front of them if they were to qualify, as there remained only two practice periods for both the 250 and 350 cc races. Dipl. Ing. Wolf conducted much of the testing himself. He was actually seen out on the mountain section of the circuit one morning, prior to breakfast, in shirt-sleeve order and with trousers rolled up to just below the knees, testing one of the triples at well over 100 mph – and with no crash hat!

After both Wünsche and Felgenheier had successfully completed their initial laps and qualified, disaster reared its ugly head – young Felgenheier crashed heavily whilst returning from an unofficial course-learning trip. This left only Wünsche to take part in the races. Although he retired on the larger model, on the 250 twin, he put up a creditable performance – both in terms of speed and reliability – to finish third, at an average speed of 81.34 mph.

By the next round in the World Championship, in Holland, modifications had been made to the cylinder finning on the three-cylinder models. The fins were now square on the two upright cylinders,

DKW camp at the 1956 Isle of Man TT

and much deeper than previously on all three pots. The outer head fins on the upright cylinder had been cast at an angle to assist the passage of air through the finning. After completing practice, however, it was decided not to contest the race.

So it was for the majority of the 1953 season, with more retirements and non-starts than finishes. The only bright note was the excellent riding of new boy Hobl.

However, as a company, DKW had done well on the commercial front, and by the beginning of 1954, the workforce had more than doubled compared with 1950, 10,000 workers being employed on all aspects of two- and four-wheeled production. Therefore, the company was on a much stronger financial footing, which meant that there was more support available for the race shop.

Moreover, in early 1954, a man was to appear on the scene who was to have a considerable influence upon future events at the Ingolstadt company, on both the production and racing fronts. His name was Robert Eberan von Eberhorst. Originally a student of the Vienna Technical College and a genuine motorcycle enthusiast during the late 1920s, he later joined Auto Union at Chemnitz in the 1930s, becoming an assistant on the development side to the legendary Professor Ferdinand Porsche. After the war, von Eberhorst went to work in England, where his

appointments included periods at the Aston Martin and BRM car organizations. In late 1953, however, he decided to return to his homeland once more, where he joined DKW as Technical Director. He was also given responsibility for the racing programme, and the resultant changes showed what a wise move this was.

Quickly deciding to concentrate efforts upon the 350 three-cylinder model, von Eberhorst scrapped the 250 twin. He also opted to reorganize the racing development team and put Dipl. Ing. Helmut Görg (who had first joined DKW in 1930) in charge of the day-to-day running of the racing section.

One of Görg's first tasks was to dismantle a complete triple and then redraw, in full, the original blueprints! The redesign which followed showed a host of changes, including a strengthened crankcase, minus the fins which had previously made a section of it appear like an additional cylinder. Another alteration was a redesigned cylinder liner.

The crankshaft, pressed together from six separate sections, was truly a work of engineering brilliance. To avoid wasted space and achieve the required crankcase compression, there were extremely narrow clearances for the slender, highly-polished connecting rods and full-circle flywheels

for a higher degree of pumping effect. As an example of the extra efficiency, Wolf had obtained a 48-per-cent balance factor, but Görg managed to increase this to 62 per cent.

Both big- and small-ends comprised caged needle bearings, and the forged, two-ring Mahle pistons were made of Sintal with American steel rings. The depth of these rings was originally 0.75 mm, but Görg increased this figure to 1 mm. It had been found that the ultra-thin rings had tended to become caught on the ports and, in addition, had a tendency to flutter (vibrate). Also in the Wolf era, deflector-type pistons had been used, but Görg immediately turned to the more-or-less flat type which today are standard ware for the modern two-stroke. To match these, he adopted new cylinder heads incorporating a squish area.

A trio of SS1 Dell'Ortos supplied the fuel. Those feeding the pair of vertical cylinders shared a common float chamber, while the horizontal cylinder's carburettor had its own. In fact, together with the correct shape and length of expansion boxes, the positioning of the float chambers was discovered by Görg to be the most critical of all the engine's performance factors.

During early testing with the 'new' engine, Helmut Görg soon discovered that, although the result of his redesign had generally been successful,

The hydraulically-operated rear brake of Cecil Sandford's works DKW, which he rode to third place in the 1956 Junior TT

the horizontal cylinder still refused to generate as much power as either of the vertical pots. To cure this, its designer burned a considerable amount of midnight oil before the output was up to the required level.

The début of the Görg 350 came at a German national meeting at the Nürburgring in late May. Compared with the Wolf engine, maximum rpm had been reduced from around 12,000 to a shade under 10,500 in order to gain piston reliability. There were now five, instead of four, gear ratios, larger and more powerful brakes, and leading-link front forks. The frame itself remained largely unchanged. Even though a trio of the revised bikes (ridden by Hofmann, Hobl and new boy Bodmer) took the first three places, their race speeds and lap times did not match those of the NSU Rennmax twins, which dominated the 250 category. Helmut Görg decided, therefore, that more development was needed before making an entry into the classic arena.

This was made at the Belgian GP in early July, where the machines showed considerable modification. In an attempt to reduce weight, the heavy six-cylinder, car-type magneto, fitted since the original prototype of 1952, was discarded in favour of battery/coil ignition, with a triple contact-breaker assembly driven from an extension of the offside end of the crankshaft. The three carburettors were now equipped with air slides which operated separately through cables from a tiny, triple-lever cluster mounted close to the handlebar clutch lever.

Of the three 'Deeks', only the machine ridden by Wünsche survived the race to take third place, showing that the design lacked the outright speed and reliability of the latest Moto Guzzis. In fact, the most notable feature of the DKW in Belgium was the controversy which surrounded the weird-looking number plate-cum-streamlining. This was deemed illegal by FIM officials, who said it contravened existing regulations. Although the race officials allowed them to be used, they were banned the following week in Holland, where the only DKW finisher was Hofmann in fifth spot.

After that, none of the Ingolstadt bikes raced that season. Instead, Görg and his team retreated to their workshop for another intensive development session.

From then on, until the beginning of the 1955 season, the race shop was a hive of activity. The result was a much-improved machine that not only produced over 40 bhp for the first time, but also offered increased reliability and superior handling.

The engine now ran at a compression ratio of 12:1, with usable power available from between 6800 and 11,000 rpm. During early track testing with the revised power unit, it had been discovered that even when changing down with the engine revolutions soaring to around 15,000 rpm, nothing had fallen to pieces. This had led Görg to realize that his basics were right, but what was needed was to create and harness usable power – which is exactly what he achieved. Another move was to make the engine run cleaner – the earlier Wolf motor employed a 16:1 petroil mixture, but Görg steadily decreased this to 25:1, through better engineering and the use of a heavier grade of lubricant.

Although the actual weight of the power unit remained the same, the whole machine now weighed 145 kg (320 lb) with streamlining. Although considerably heavier than previously, and weighing

more than the competition – for example, the 1954 championship Guzzi weighed 118 kg (260 lb) – the latest DKW was preferred by its riders over the earlier models. This was not only because of improved power characteristics and reliability, but also because the extra weight had got rid of several problems which had been features of the earlier, ultra-lightweight triples.

Finally, there were now much larger, stronger and more powerful hydraulically-operated brakes on both wheels. The earlier 'stoppers' had not only proved borderline in their ability, but the drums had been prone to cracking. The new brakes were 215 mm in diameter, and each wheel had two separate units back to back. These were connected to a master cylinder operated by the foot pedal, which applied both and automatically supplied the correct bias to the front and rear wheels. A hand lever enabled the rider to increase the braking effect on the front wheel if required. It could be argued that DKW had invented the linked brake system used by Moto Guzzi some two decades later on their V-twin roadsters.

Another problem which had finally been eradicated was that of high-frequency vibration. During 1953 and 1954, the life of a rev-counter on one of the racing triples had often been as short as a mere 20 miles! After careful investigation, Görg

DKW's chief racing designer, Helmut Görg, (left) with fellow engineer Josef Wagner, pictured up on the mountain testing wind speeds with an anemometer, 1956 TT

discovered that the problem centred around certain vibrations which were being transmitted from the engine to the frame. He finally solved this by increasing the quality of the crankcase material and strengthening the crankshaft, but it was also found that the extra weight of the machine and modified crankcase supports combined to defeat what had formerly been one of the design's major drawbacks. As might be imagined, few riders wished to race a two-stroke vibro-massager with a super-narrow power band and no rev-counter!

Considerable time was also spent with the INA bearing company, who came up with more robust needle bearings for both the small- and big-ends. Görg even took this a stage further, using needle-roller bearings in the swinging-arm pivot from 1955.

Another problem was crankcase sealing, and much time and energy was to be expended before a satisfactory solution was finally evolved. This included the use of double-lipped seals in place of the original single-lipped components.

Other changes took place in the cylinder heads, porting, timing and, most important of all, the exhaust system. Görg employed a flat type of expansion chamber and, after many exhaustive bench tests, ascertained the optimum length and size. He was able to gain a relatively high increase in the mixture induced at certain engine revolutions – up to an amazing 80 per cent at certain points!

Another aspect of the development cycle was the use of streamlining, which the Ingolstadt team found, like Moto Guzzi and NSU, could add up to 10 mph to the maximum velocity, depending on the circuit. Well over 100 different shells were tested in a wind tunnel. However, unlike the other two marques mentioned, which raced four-strokes, DKW not only had air resistance to worry about, but also the effective cooling of three cylinders to consider.

Helmut Görg also built a single-cylinder version of the engine, initially to provide additional data on the behaviour of the horizontal cylinder, but later he decided to use it in a 125-class racer. This did not make its début until midway through the 1955 season, when it won first time out at the Sachsenring circuit, in the eastern sector of Germany.

That year, the DKW team comprised Wünsche, Hobl and new man Hans Bartl. It was Hobl who capped a much better year for the Ingolstadt équipe by taking third place in the World Championship. This was thanks to a big leap in both speed and

Sandford at speed during the 1956 Junior TT

Works rider August Hobl at Solitude, 21 July 1956. He was the most successful of all the post-war DKW racers

reliability, displayed by second places on such demanding circuits as the Nürburgring (stamina) and Spa (speed). An additional encouragement was the performance of the new 125 machine. At its classic début at Monza, in September, Hobl came home fourth, with team-mate Wünsche fifth.

Hobl also took the 350 German National Championship on the redesigned triple, to give DKW its most successful season yet in post-war racing.

This success did not stop further development, however, and Görg again spent the winter months on painstaking work to further refine both the 350

triple and 125 single. By the beginning of the 1956 season, the larger machine provided a reliable 46 bhp at 9700 rpm, which meant over 140 mph, while the 125 offered 17 bhp at 9700 rpm – 110 mph out on the road. Obviously, the full 'dustbin'-type streamlining played a vital role in achieving these speeds.

Also in early 1956, the former Moto Guzzi rider and team manager, Fergus Anderson, tested the 350 DKW at Monza. Although Görg was highly impressed with the Scot, nothing ever came of this, as Anderson was killed at Floreffe in Belgium before the classic season got under way.

However, another British rider did join DKW that year. This was the 1952 125 cc World Champion, Cecil Sandford. Unfortunately, probably due to the massive down-turn in sales of DKW's production roadsters at the time, neither Sandford nor Hobl rode in all six rounds of the 350 cc world title series.

That said, the team still put in some impressive performances in a number of events, including the Dutch TT, Belgian GP, German GP and the Italian GP. DKW's sole entry in the Isle of Man TT was Sandford, who came home fourth, proving how reliable the triple had become.

At the season's end, Hobl repeated his third place in the 350 cc championship table, with Sandford fourth.

The final round of the 1956 World Championship took place in early September at Monza, Italy. Nobody knew it at the time, but this was to prove DKW's classic swan-song – never again were the screaming triples nor, for that matter, the tiny horizontal singles to appear in a Grand Prix. However, it was not the team's final appearance. This came later that month at the international Avus races, held over the steeply-banked Berlin circuit on Sunday 16 September.

Hobl made it an event to remember with pride by giving DKW victory in the 350 race at an amazing average speed of 116.5 mph. Thus, the curtain came down on one of Germany's truly great racing motorcycle marques.

5
Fath – one man against the odds

Helmut Fath was born in 1930, and his first motor-cycle came in 1946 when, at the age of 16, he purchased a well-worn, pre-war BMW 250 single. In those days, Fath was living just outside Mannheim, working at an experimental laboratory where research into high-altitude aviation was undertaken. He had begun there at the age of 14 in the dark days of 1944, when the whole of Germany was under great strain with the Allies attacking on all sides.

When the war finally came to an end in the following year, the young Fath was kept on at the plant after it was taken over by the victorious Allied forces. Serving an apprenticeship as a precision engineer, he stayed on until he was 18. By that time, Helmut Fath had been converted to the ranks of motorcycle enthusiasts and had owned a string of machinery. This interest led him to quit the aviation industry and go to work (for less money!) in a motorcycle dealership. With his precision engineering background, Fath was soon given the more specialized jobs, such as building up BMW crank-shafts and inserting valve seats, for example.

The following year, 1949, he took part in his first competitive event. This was a trial in which he rode a twin-piston German Triumph (TWN) two-stroke.

With money in short supply, his real interest – road racing – had to wait. It was to be three long years before his ambition on this front was finally realized. This came in the shape of a standard, road-going, BMW pushrod flat-twin, which was tuned and fitted with a sidecar.

This effort proved two things: the machine was simply not fast enough, and neither was its pilot!

For 1953, the BMW chassis was retained, but the engine was subjected to a vast amount of tuning work. Having several years of experience on this type of unit was a distinct advantage, but the problem of finance, or lack of it, remained. As he was only able to race in his holidays, Fath took part in only three meetings that year. However, a victory

Helmut Fath, World Sidecar Champion, brilliant engineer and gifted tuner

was taken at each of these, with the result that the name Helmut Fath joined the Senior category in German classification. This meant that although Fath could only race within the German borders, he was able to take part in international meetings.

His new status posed another problem, however – the home-tuned pushrod BMW, although quick enough to win races in the Junior class, was totally outclassed among the superior opposition which he now faced.

Therefore, taking the chance to sell his original outfit, Helmut Fath ordered one of the small batch of

Above

The Fath fuel-injected, dohc, 500 cc, four-cylinder racing engine, circa 1967

Rennsport BMWs that the Munich factory was building at the time (see Chapter 3). Unfortunately, a financial hiccup prevented him from obtaining his overhead-cam BMW, with the result that he did not compete in a single race during 1954.

However, in December that year, he finally managed to obtain a solo Rennsport model – one of the 1954 batch – and set about converting it to sidecar use. This included building a special frame, converting the brakes to hydraulic operation and constructing a superbly-crafted aluminium fairing.

For the next four years, it was a case of steady and ever-improving form, and in 1959, Helmut Fath finally launched himself as a serious contender for the World Sidecar Championship when he finished the season in fifth spot, partnered by Alfred Wohlgemuth on a BMW Rennsport outfit.

The year 1960 was full of glory, for the duo totally dominated the title series, winning four out of the five rounds, and placing second in the other, the Dutch TT.

Typical of the man behind the name, Fath not only won the Isle of Man TT, but also helped his rival, Pip Harris, to gain second place. Harris had blown his BMW engine in practice and, to his surprise, Fath had waded in and completely rebuilt the Rennsport engine, using new spares, pieces from Pip's old engine and parts from Jack Beeton's BMW engine. The work took the best part of two days, and Helmut's only reward was Pip's second position –

true sportsmanship, indeed.

The following year, 1961, Fath and Wohlgemuth looked all set to retain their world title, following a runaway victory during the first round in Spain when they lapped the entire field.

Then came tragedy. A week later, at the international Eifelrennen meeting over the Nürburgring circuit, the World Champions crashed in appalling conditions of heavy mist and rain. This left Wohlgemuth dead and Fath badly injured. His injuries included a broken leg, ankle and hand, and they effectively sidelined Helmut for five long years.

Most men would have given up, but Helmut Fath was nothing if not determined. His burning ambition was to make a comeback – and with his own engine.

Once he had recovered from the effects of the accident that had claimed his passenger and friend, Fath set about designing, building and finally testing

his own across-the-frame, four-cylinder, double-overhead-camshaft racing engine. This was known as the URS, after the village of Ursenbach where he had made his home.

The URS design was really a pair of side-by-side parallel twins, coupled together by a countershaft driven from the crankshaft between cylinders 1 and 2 and 3 and 4. The firing order was 1-4-2-3, and the engine featured a central timing chain. The crankshaft ran on six main bearings, with caged roller big-ends and phosphor-bronze small-ends in the titanium con-rods. The lubrication system included a combined oil cooler and filter. The bore and stroke measurements of the new engine were 60×44 mm, the ultra-short-stroke unit giving useful power between 8000 and 13,500 rpm. Even from the first prototype, the URS was a very high-revving unit, and it was a remarkable technical achievement to be able to control the valves up to 15,000 rpm with a conventional two-valves-per-cylinder layout.

Credit for this went to Fath's partner, Dr Peter Kuhn (formerly a lecturer at Heidelburg University). He had designed the cam profile and valve spring rates to match — the special Swedish wire used for these springs was later supplied by Fath for use in various other engines.

The valves themselves were large in size — 34 mm inlet, and 30 mm exhaust — and were splayed at 67

Overleaf
Fath URS works rider John Blanchard during the 500 cc Ulster GP, 19 August 1967

Below
Fath leads Harris (right) and Seeley at Brands Hatch, 29 May 1967

degrees. As a result, twin 10 mm sparking plugs were fitted in each cylinder and, unusually, these were mounted vertically, as otherwise there was not enough room for the valves.

Fuel was injected directly into the ports by a Bosch injector mounted between the wide-angle upper frame tubes, above and behind the engine unit. The injector had come from a 1.5-litre Borgward car, and a divided cable from the twistgrip moved the single flat throttle plate to regulate the fuel supply. Although contemporary press reports claimed 80 bhp for the engine, Fath laughed at this and said his dynamometer had told only him – and he was keeping it a secret!

Fath made his comeback in May 1966 at the West German Grand Prix, staged at Hockenheim. His reappearance five years after the Nürburgring accident, and the new engine, created a sensation. Unfortunately, he retired after just three laps when lying sixth. This was the start of a series of problems which its creator discovered with the URS engine during that first season. In fact, Fath hardly finished a race.

At the beginning of 1967, it appeared to be the same story, the URS seeming not to have enough power. However, at the West German GP at Hockenheim, Fath took an instant lead from the start, but despite building up a four-second lead over Klaus Enders' BMW, he was forced out near the end with a broken gearbox selector mechanism.

It was also during that year that the URS engine was first considered for solo use, with the news that John Blanchard was considering racing one mounted in a frame built by Colin Seeley. At the time, Blanchard stated: 'I think the engine may be better for a solo than a sidecar, and is now giving good power.' Unlike the sidecar power unit, the solo engine was fitted with carburettors and had magnesium-alloy, instead of aluminium, castings.

By the time of the 1967 TT, Helmut Fath's home-built, four-cylinder URS outfit was outspeeding the fastest short-stroke BMWs – no mean achievement. Furthermore, it appeared that if he could achieve reliability and improve handling, he would once again dominate the class.

It was then revealed that although the engine had repeatedly suffered from fractures of the long bolts clamping the crankcase halves to the central driving sprockets, some of Fath's engine failures had been due to the inability of the battery/coil ignition system to cope with the unorthodox crankshaft layout. Therefore, to stabilize the ignition, Fath had reverted to a magneto.

The difficulty had been due to his choice of crankpin spacing. Instead of having all four in one plane (two up, two down), Fath had spaced them like the points of a compass to achieve smoother running. This gave firing intervals of 90, 180, 270 and 360 degrees. However, at the peak power point of 14,000 rpm, the 90-degree interval had given the contact-breaker precious little time to do its job. It was hoped that the new system would solve this problem.

Both Fath and Dr Kuhn spent time in England with John Blanchard at the Seeley works in Belvedere, Kent. Late July saw the Seeley-framed Fath four solo racer completed, and a particularly neat effort it looked, too. Many of the cycle parts – except the full duplex cradle frame – were the same as used on the production Seeley 7R and G50 ohc single-cylinder racers.

Fath and Blanchard both appeared with their respective fours at the Hutchinson 100 at Brands Hatch on 13 August. Two weeks later, the duo appeared at Scarborough on Saturday 26 August, when Fath and his passenger, Wolfgang Kallaugh, scored an impressive win over the World Champion Klaus Enders.

Blanchard, however, fell at Mere Hairpin, putting himself out of the running. There followed a row, with Blanchard being withdrawn from the Snetterton and Oulton Park meetings in the following two days of the Bank Holiday meetings. This followed a stormy exchange between Seeley and Blanchard at Snetterton over the bike being fitted with a Lockheed disc brake before Scarborough, without Seeley's permission. The result was that Blanchard was dropped as development rider and would not be allowed to ride the machine any more that season.

A couple of weeks later, following discussions between Seeley and Fath, the prospects of work continuing on their four-cylinder racer brightened. However, Fath had elected to leave all decisions concerning the project to his partner in the design and development of the URS, Dr Kuhn.

In any case, the Seeley–Fath co-operation didn't last beyond the end of the season, and for the future, the Fath team chose to use the Metisse chassis made by the Rickman brothers of New Milton in Hampshire. John Blanchard returned to ride the URS-Metisse solo – and in a supreme irony, it was fitted with the very Lockheed disc brake set-up that had caused the rift between him and Seeley.

Blanchard gave the machine its first outing at Brands Hatch in January 1968, when he was principally concerned with testing the brakes and suspen-

sion, watched by Derek Rickman and Mike Vaughan of Lockheed. Afterwards, all decided that they were very happy with the machine's performance, but thought that a little more experimentation was needed to sort out the rear suspension.

More tests were carried out before Blanchard and the URS-Metisse were entered in the season's first classic, the West German GP at the Nürburgring. This was anything but a successful début, as Blanchard crashed *twice*. The machine was then offered to John Hartle, who rode it at Hockenheim on 12 May.

If the solo plans didn't proceed as intended, Fath's own racing efforts certainly did. At the Nürburgring, he and Wolfgang Kallaugh took the flag at the front of the field – Fath's first Grand Prix victory since his win in Spain in April 1961. What a sweet taste of success it was for a man who had not only made a successful comeback, but built the engine of his machine into the bargain!

Then came the Isle of Man TT and a fourth, followed by a fifth in the Dutch TT, a retirement in Belgium and then a couple of victories in Belgium and the final round at Hockenheim. The last event was to have taken place at the Italian GP at Monza, but as the sidecar event was cancelled, by FIM

Fath in action during his World Championship year, 1968 – the first, and only, man in history to win the sidecar title using an engine designed and built by himself

decree, it was contested at Hockenheim, with the final of the German National Championship in October.

Before Hockenheim, both Fath and Georg Auerbacher had gained 21 points each, while TT winner Siegfried Schauzu was four points astern, but still in with a chance. With so much at stake, Fath took a desperate gamble after official practice finished. Dissatisfied with his engine, he fitted a completely new short-stroke unit which had not been raced before, but which had been showing promising results on the test-bed. Would it last the race? Fath commented grimly before the start: 'The only way to find out is to use it.'

The gamble paid off. Before the first corner, Fath and passenger Wolfgang Kallaugh already had a tremendous lead, and even the super-fast BMW of ex-World Champion Enders was unable to get a tow in the slipstream of the flying URS. A wet and slippery track failed to deter a determined Fath, then 39 years old, and at the end of the second lap, his lead

The Fath-designed, flat-four, two-stroke engine which made its début in 1972

was 6.6 seconds. This doubled in the next two circuits to take him out of reach of everyone – a lead which was maintained until the end. The 15-lap, 63.15-mile race was won at an average speed of 98.55 mph, with a fastest lap (by Fath) of 100.72 mph, breaking Enders' previous record.

Helmut Fath made history because, up to that time, nobody had ever won a world championship on a home-built machine. Strangely, when defending the title in the following year, the results turned out almost in reverse, with wins in France, Holland and Belgium, a third in the Isle of Man, and a retirement in Germany. With two rounds to go and leading the championship, he crashed in Finland, preventing his participation in the final round in Ulster – Klaus Enders took the title for BMW.

For 1969, Fath built a larger version of his four – initially for British short circuits, where it was popular to race larger-capacity outfits. the 68 × 51.5 mm bore and stroke gave 748 cc, compared with the smaller unit's 60 × 44 mm. Much longer con-rods were used, together with different cylinders and larger valves. The aim was to produce an engine with tremendous low-down punch, rather than power at high revs, and Fath hoped that a four-speed gearbox would be adequate. In this, he was proved wrong, as like the 500, the 750 needed at least five speeds.

At long last, however, the 500 solo racer began to shine. Ridden by veteran Karl Hoppe, the URS-Metisse dominated many of the early-seasonal Continental internationals. Perhaps his finest performance came just a week after his first victory – the Eifelrennen at the end of April – when Hoppe won the 500 class of the non-championship Austrian GP at Salzburg. Under ideal racing conditions, in front of a crowd of 28,000 spectators, no one could keep up with Hoppe, who shot away from the start and won as he pleased. Not only was his race speed a record, but he also shaved 0.7 seconds off Giacomo Agostini's lap record, which had been set on an MV four in 1967.

Then, to prove that his early form was no fluke, Hoppe finished a fine second in the West German GP at Hockenheim, behind Agostini's MV. Sadly, however, Hoppe did not contest the remainder of the classics. This was a great pity, as except for MV, 1969 saw the URS emerge as the most serious World-Championship contender in the 500 cc class.

Although there were several URS engines in existence, there were still only two machines: Fath's own outfit and the Metisse solo ridden by Hoppe. Fath had also received help from several British companies, including Reynolds Tubes, Automotive Products, Renold Chain, Duckhams Oil (the main sponsor) and Dunlop, who had developed a special 4.00 × 12 tyre for the outfit. Both types of the URS engine were now giving useful power between 9000 and 13,000 rpm, and transmission was via a Norton box with a six-speed Schafleitner cluster.

The Bosch fuel injection on the sidecar engine now had twin air intakes instead of the single intake previously used. Moreover, a final solution had been found to beat the ignition problems which had remained, despite the adoption of a fully-transistorized system. The answer was found by fitting a separate coil for each cylinder and making a special contact-breaker with four sets of points spaced at 45, 90, 135 and 180 degrees. Since each cylinder had two spark plugs, the coils were double-ended to furnish pairs of sparks simultaneously.

Things looked bright, indeed, but then Fath sustained a broken leg in Finland on 12 August. While he was recuperating, towards the end of the month, there came the news that the Fath team had been purchased by Friedl Münch with American backing, as related in Chapter 10. The Münch/Fath tie-up eventually took place in May 1970, and because all of his machinery had been taken over, it was not until much later that Fath resumed manufacturing. During 1970–1, he was strictly a tuner, although during 1971, he was said to be one of the top Yamaha tuners around — even the 250 World Champion was a customer.

In the middle of 1973 came the first news that Fath, then aged 43, was thinking of a possible comeback. At his forest hideout near Heidelburg, Fath was busy constructing a brand-new four-cylinder outfit. Furthermore, not only did he have plans for a racing return himself, but he hoped to have a spare engine for Billie Nelson to race in solo events.

This time, his design was for a watercooled, disc-valve, two-stroke flat-four, which many wrongly considered at the time to be a development of the König. In fact, any resemblance to the König began and ended with the flat-four cylinder layout. In any case, in the early 1960s, Fath's original scheme had been to build a watercooled flat-four (albeit a four-stroke) before ultimately opting for the across-the-frame layout of the URS. The reason he had not built the original design was said to be the reluctance of BMW to provide certain parts, notably the transmission, on which the design depended.

Unlike the König, Fath's two-stroke had a longitudinal position for the crankshaft and an integral six-speed gearbox with the clutch at the rear of the crankcase, in a similar manner to the BMW design — but with a pair of bevel gears coupling the output shaft to the left-hand side-mounted sprocket for the chain final drive, turning it through an angle of 90 degrees. Another departure from König practice was the oil supply to the big-end which, on the Berlin company's engine, was by a direct shower of petroil. Fath devised a belt-driven pump, controlled by the throttle, which dribbled a supply of straight oil to the big-ends, main bearings and disc bearings. Caged needle rollers were used for both the big- and small-ends.

With a capacity of 495 cc (56 × 50 mm), the Fath four had aluminium-alloy cylinders with Nickasil

The 'stroker' unit in a sidecar chassis, showing the exhaust system and carburettors to advantage

bores. Originally, Yamaha pistons were used, but these were soon replaced by purpose-built units, carrying only a single ring each.

A unique feature of the Fath design was that each cylinder casting incorporated half the crankcase, so that the crank chambers themselves were also watercooled. There was no water pump of the type fitted to many watercooled 'strokers', but as on Bultacos and MZ, the thermo-siphon system was used, water entering the underside of the cylinders and leaving them at the top.

Fuel was supplied by a quartet of separate carburettors – 34 mm Japanese Mikunis. Because Fath used four carburettors, this called for four small disc valves instead of the König's one, but like the König, the drive to these was by toothed rubber belt. Also unlike the König, Fath used four separate expansion chambers in an attempt to extract the maximum possible power output – 112 bhp at 12,200 rpm. The exhausts ran from the top of the engine and back under the rider's legs. To prevent him from being burned, they were coated with a baked-on finish, and as Billie Nelson was to remark; 'It's really amazing. You can touch them and not get burned even after a long race.'

At first, the ignition was by a Bosch flywheel magneto, with the generator incorporating a pair of ignition coils, two pulse coils and three more for the water pump, fuel pump and tachometer. However, this system proved too heavy, and thereafter a battery was installed for current, and only a pulse unit was fitted to the front of the crankshaft.

At 44, Helmut Fath was not sure if he would race again, but May 1974 saw Fath's new four in action for the first time, at the West German GP at Hockenheim in solo trim with Billie Nelson up. Ready to race, but without fuel, the Fath weighed only 130 kg (286 lb), some 25 kg (55 lb) less than the comparable Yamaha or Suzuki 500 fours – but there were problems.

The power proved exceptional, but not so the handling. The frame had been constructed in only ten days, after the original builder failed to come up with the goods, and Fath freely admitted that he was not a frame specialist. The problems centred around the swinging arm, which was whipping so badly at Hockenheim that it caused Nelson's ultimate retirement. There were also early problems with the transmission system.

The IoM TT was given a miss, and the machine's next outing was at the international meeting at Raalte in Holland, where again it showed a tremendous turn of speed. However, trouble with the

Billie Nelson on the 500 Fath four leads Gerrit Valdink (Suzuki TR500), Dutch TT, 16 June 1974

throttle linkage slowed Nelson in the race, although he kept going to finish fourth.

The next race was the Dutch TT at Assen where, in the 350 race, Nelson clocked up a fourth on his Yamaha. At the start of the 500 race, however, the Fath four oiled a plug. By the time it had been changed and Nelson got started, the leaders had already come round to complete one lap. He followed them down the straight and, to his amazement, caught them up easily. He said afterwards that he could have passed them easily, but for two things. Firstly, he was not totally confident in the machine's handling on the very fast curve towards the end of the straight, and secondly he himself hated people who indulged in what he called 'dicing with me

when I'm lapping them.' The riders whom Billie Nelson was in danger of catching in this way were none other than the trio of Barry Sheene (Suzuki), Giacomo Agostini (Yamaha) and Phil Read (MV Agusta)!

Besides the evident speed, Nelson was impressed by the smoothness of the engine, describing it as 'just like a big electric motor'. He thought the wide spread of usable power from 8000 to 13,000 rpm was particularly impressive, and development continued apace throughout the summer of 1974, with an excellent understanding existing between builder and rider.

However, on Sunday 8 September, all this was shattered. Billie Nelson, the man who had once been known as 'Mr Consistency' on the Grand Prix circuit, died after he crashed during the 250 race at Opatija in the Yugoslav Grand Prix. He crashed on a 125 mph left-hander at one of the highest points of

the closed road circuit on the Adriatic coast. The Yamaha went into the crowd and a spectator was seriously injured, while Nelson suffered severe chest injuries and died after an operation in hospital at nearby Rijeka.

The 33-year-old Nelson, from Eckington, Derbyshire, had begun racing in 1958 and made his Continental début six years later in West Germany. He combined solo racing and sidecar passengering for several years. It was a crash while racing as passenger with Fath in 1969, during the Finnish GP, which ruined not only Fath's chances of retaining his world title, but also Nelson's hopes of taking the Bill Hannah-sponsored Paton twin to second place in the 500 cc World Championship behind Agostini.

Fath and Nelson had been firm friends as well as colleagues, and his death was a cruel blow. Following the accident, Fath decided to make a return to the sidecar scene, the engine from Nelson's solo being

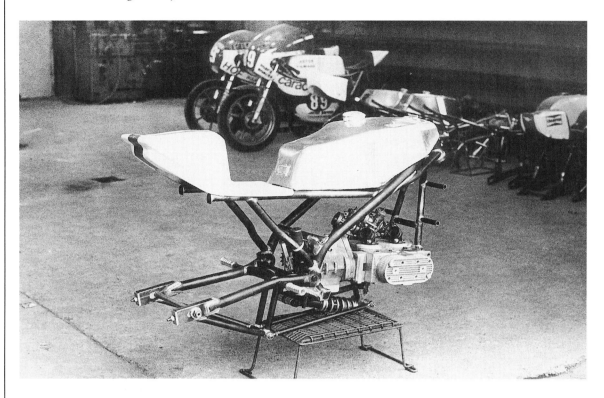

Fath engine in Nico Bakker frame, September 1977

built into a special three-wheeler for Siegfried Schauzu. However, Fath was far from happy with the outfit (it was not of his design) and, in May 1975, said: 'It is far too big and the width of the sidecar alone loses me 10–15 bhp.'

By then, Fath had almost completed a new engine which he said would produce even more horsepower, and he hoped that the rest of the outfit would be modified. Early results were far from impressive, however, with only one placing in the top ten at any of the Grands Prix that year, when the ARO-Fath finished at Hockenheim.

For 1976, the sidecar team consisted of two pairings: Schauzu and Kallaugh, plus newcomer Heinz Schilling partnered by passenger Rolf Gundel. In the very first round at Le Mans, in France, Schilling managed a third place, with Schauzu coming home eighth. At the Salzburgring, in Austria, Schauzu came in third, although Schilling had to retire.

Displaying their greatly-improved reliability, both crews finished the punishing IoM TT, Schauzu in fourth and Schilling in sixth place. Then, in Holland, Schilling was fifth, with Schauzu in tenth place, while on the following weekend, in Belgium the ARO-Fath teams made it third and fourth – Schilling and Schauzu. Neither team competed in the

Czech GP at Brno, and the season ended with a ninth for Schauzu at the Nürburgring. As a result, Schauzu and Kallaugh came fifth overall in the year's championship table.

In the same year, Alex George, the Scottish solo racer, then based in Holland, rode Helmut Fath's four-cylinder 'stroker' solo in the Czech Grand Prix. George's Suzuki four had been sidelined with a broken idler gear, so he took over the Fath bike, the chassis of which remained untouched since Billie Nelson last raced it. He found the machine to be around 10 mph slower than the all-conquering (but at that time, none too reliable) Suzukis, and a match for them on acceleration. He led for most of the first lap, but gradually dropped back and retired when he grounded one of the plug caps.

For 1977, the ARO team was again reorganized. Schauzu left to race his own Yamaha, while Schilling was provided with a new ARO-Yamaha. Then, after the season had started, Werner Schwarzel (second in 1976 on a König) was brought into the team with passenger Huber and took over one of the vacant ARO-Fath outfits.

Schwarzel's first finish was at the Dutch TT, with a third, following which he demonstrated his own superb skill and the potential of the Fath engine to the full by winning the next round in Belgium on the super-fast Spa circuit. He then retired in Czechoslovakia, but won the final round at Silverstone to finish third in the world series. This was an amazing result when you consider that the team had only finished in three of the seven rounds!

This result was to prove the pinnacle of achievement by Fath's flat-four, even though it did not appear so at the time, and the man himself was still interested in both the sidecar and solo classes at world level.

At the end of 1977, South African Jon Ekerold, later to be World 350 cc Champion in 1980 on a Bimota-Yamaha, was tipped to be rider of a new machine powered by a Fath flat-four. Fath had been so impressed with Ekerold's riding ability, when he saw him in action at the end-of-season Nürburgring international, that he offered to let him have one of his 500 engines and also to prepare Ekerold's 250 and 350 Yamaha power units.

Ekerold soon had a Nico Bakker frame with monoshock suspension constructed to house the Fath four, but in the end, he decided to concentrate on riding his pair of Yamahas. The Fath four was shelved, this time never to reappear. With the speed and reliability of the new breed of Japanese four-cylinder 'strokers', a private effort, even with as gifted a tuner as Fath, simply could not compete.

In the 1978 world sidecar series, Fath was to suffer yet more disappointment. Schwarzel still proved almost unbeatable, but his two victories at Assen and the Nürburgring, with a second at Mugello, in Italy, and a sixth in Nogaro, France, simply were not enough to stop Rolf Biland and his passenger, Englishman Kenny Williams, from taking the title with their Yamaha-powered BEO machine. What a machine it was, too – quite simply the most radical interpretation of the sidecar construction rules that had ever been seen.

It appeared to be a perfectly natural development of a line that began earlier in the mid 1970s. Parallelogram suspension had appeared when sidecar racing constructors started using racing-car suspension and wheels on conventional, short-wheelbase outfits. However, this line of development, as racing outfits grew steadily more like three-wheeled racing cars, was speedily terminated when Biland produced his BEO *tricar*, which was so radical that it forced the FIM into creating *two* world sidecar classes for 1979: the B2A for conventional outfits, and the B2B for the new breed. Regulations were hastily redrafted to outlaw racing-car suspensions and steering systems, and this meant a total reappraisal for everyone connected with the three-wheel racing fraternity. The result was a new breed of long-wheelbase, fully-enclosed racing three-wheelers – now commonly referred to as *worms*.

This was the last straw for Fath, who by now had not only given up the idea of making a return himself, but with the split championship in 1979 had finally decided to call it a day in his bid to be a combination of world champion and one-man motorcycle manufacturer.

It was the end of an era that had spanned 20 years, during which he had been World Champion in 1960, fought back from serious injury to win back the championship in 1968 with his own four-cylinder dohc engine, then had everything taken from him in the Münch deal in 1970, before coming back *again* with a completely new design to join the contest once more. In the process, some of his closest friends and racing partners had lost their lives through accidents, and it is unlikely that any other man in the history of motorcycle sport has ever suffered such peaks of triumph and depths of despair as Helmut Fath. In overcoming the setbacks, his character can be summed up in one world – fighter.

6
Horex – singles and twins

Today, because of its association with the classic four-stroke single-cylinder roadster concept of the 1940s and 1950s, the Horex is widely sought after by enthusiasts and collectors alike in modern Germany. However, the Bad Homburg company also had another side – both before and after World War 2, it took part, with varying success, in road-racing events throughout the Fatherland and abroad.

The founder of Horex was Friedrich Kleeman who, together with his son Fritz, showed considerable entrepreneurial skills in a number of successful business ventures during the early 1920s. Kleeman

senior was also the main shareholder of the Columbus Motorenwerke in Oberusel, which manufactured auxiliary engines for bicycles, as well as larger units for motorcycles.

In 1923, the father-and-son team founded another company, with the intention of designing and building complete motorcycles. This enterprise was centred on a former manufacturing company owned by the Kleeman family. It was given the name Horex – from the first two letters of Homburg which were added to the brand name Rex, which the previous company had used.

The first Horex motorcycle appeared in 1924. Not surprisingly, the new firm chose a Columbus engine, a 248 cc pushrod single, with hand-operated, three-speed gearbox. The frame was typical of the era with

The original 500 Horex parallel-twin prototype in May 1951, sohc and 30 bhp

Works rider Friedl Schön with the 'new' Horex twin, 17 April 1952. Much revised, it featured double overhead camshafts

its simple tubular steel construction, flat tank and sprung saddle. The front fork employed a rocker arm, which was suspended on a central spring and incorporated a single friction damper absorber.

Not only did these early Horex machines sell well to the public, but they were raced with considerable success, too. The interest in motorcycle sport stemmed from the fact that Fritz Kleeman was also a well-known racing motorist and motorcyclist, and with the new 248 cc ohv single, suitably tuned and stripped for action, he soon had Horex competing in races throughout Germany. There was a trio of works riders – Phillip Karrer, Henry Veit and, of course, Fritz Kleeman (in true pioneering spirit).

Horex designs soon proved successful, not only in racing, but also in long-distance trials. Perhaps the greatest success of the original trio came in the first race ever staged over the legendary Nürburgring circuit. Fritz Kleeman finished third on a 596 cc Horex, the cylinder of which had been bored out to

give 675 cc, against the might of factory teams from the likes of Norton, Harley Davidson and New Imperial.

By 1930, the Bad Homburg marque was established on a firm commercial footing, with both production and profits soaring. Columbus engines were also doing well, not only being used by Horex, but also by other German marques, such as AWD, Tornax and Victoria.

In the early 1930s, Horex and Columbus merged their interests by moving engine production from Oberusel to Bad Homburg. This heralded even greater success, for the new grouping employed the brilliant designer Hermann Reeb.

It was Reeb who created a sensation in 1932 when he designed a pair of large-capacity vertical twins of 598 and 796 cc with chain-driven ohc. The drive to the overhead camshaft was on the offside of the engine, enclosed in a large alloy casting which dominated that side of the power unit. This led to the design's one major disadvantage – the spark plug on the timing side was obstructed by this vast housing.

There had been vertical twins before, of course, but not like this. Far be it for me to claim a first for the Bad Homburg factory, but although Triumph

Swiss Grand Prix, 17–18 May 1952. Friedl Schön aboard the 500 Horex twin during practice

and Edward Turner are today universally credited with the conception of the modern vertical twin, perhaps Horex and Hermann Reeb could have argued that they were there some four years earlier . . .

On the racing front, Horex had continued to participate with success. In the late 1920s, Franz Islinger and Josef Klein garnered considerable success on the 248 and 498 cc singles. Then, at the 1929 German Grand Prix at the Nürburgring, expatriate Briton Tommy Bullus rode so effectively on one of the larger machines that only a retirement with just a few miles to go was to rob him and Horex of a famous victory. In the 1930s, Karl Braun used a supercharged version of the ohc twin to win many sidecar events, including victory in the 1935 German Sidecar Championship. Many of Braun's victories came with an engine enlarged to 980 cc.

During the mid and late 1930s, Horex continued in

a leading position, both on the race circuit and the street. Not only did it refine existing models, but it also introduced brand-new 500 and 600 cc four-valve singles.

However, as with other manufacturers' plans, the demands of the Third Reich's war machine had largely taken over by the end of the decade. The result was that, by the outbreak of war in September 1939, the Bad Homburg production facilities had been turned over totally to the needs of the military (but not to the manufacture of motorcycles).

Horex survived the conflict in far better shape than any of its rivals and, therefore, was able to resume volume production without many of the difficulties encountered by the remainder of the German motorcycle industry. Allied to this, it was doubly fortunate in being the first company to gain permission from the occupying forces to build a machine with a capacity of over 250 cc. At the time, several outsiders claimed that the Kleeman family had more than a close relationship with certain powerful Americans . . .

Horex traded under the title Horex-Columbus-Werke KG Fritz Kleeman in the years immediately after the war (although from 1953, the Columbus part was removed). In the late 1940s, Horex was authorized to build machines for police and other official duties.

This, in turn, led to the development of the best-selling Regina. It used an entirely new 342 cc (69 × 91.5 mm), semi-unit-construction, ohv single with a four-speed gearbox and simplex chain primary drive. In standard trim, the Regina produced 15 bhp at a lowly 3500 rpm. It may come as a surprise, therefore, to learn that the first post-war Horex racer was one of the 350 Reginas with a specially-tuned engine that pumped out 25 bhp at 5500 rpm, a close-ratio gearbox and several other modifications, including alloy rims and lightweight mudguards.

The race-modified roadster made its début at the Eilenriede Rennen meeting near Hanover in April 1950. However, its performance was not competitive against the pukka racing singles, such as the ohc Norton and AJS 7R 'Boy Racer', and the project was abandoned shortly afterwards.

The evident limitations of the pushrod, single-cylinder design in this new role led Horex to design a new flagship machine, one which could be used on both race track and road.

For this task, the factory's development staff opted for a twin – the first such Horex since Herman Reeb's trend-setting machine of 1932. Called the Imperator (meaning Emperor or General), the new bike first appeared in public during the spring of 1951, when a racing version appeared at the Waiblinger Dreiechsrennen road races. At the time, Horex stated that the Imperator was competing solely as part of its development programme and that design work was not complete, nor indeed had the final specification of the machine been definitely decided.

Compared to Reeb's twin, the 1951 version was much wider. Although bulky, its lines were business-like, with the drive to its ohc by chain, which ran between the cylinders. Furthermore, a lavish (for the era) use of aluminium for its generously-proportioned, unit-construction engine kept the weight down.

Also, when compared to the earlier Horex design, the new unit's symmetry of layout had the advantage of offering more equal cooling for each cylinder

Engine details of the machine used by Schön at the 1952 Swiss GP. Note aircooled clutch and hairpin valve springs

and allowing the designer to fit the spark plugs in the normal position. The central camshaft drive allowed the cam itself to be shorter, thus avoiding the possibility of flexing with its obvious effect upon valve timing.

On the debit side, however, the 1951 engine had three factors. Firstly, a four-bearing crankshaft was essential on account of the central timing valve gear; secondly, the timing chain was more difficult to assemble; and thirdly, the air passage between the two cylinders was greatly reduced.

The running gear also displayed a number of innovative features for Horex. Rather than relying on the engine unit as a stressed member (which its full unit-construction layout would have allowed), the frame was a full duplex cradle affair that enclosed the engine. However, as if to make the point that it was a prototype, the telescopic front forks and full-width alloy brake hubs appeared to be standard production Regina components. I say appeared, as, in reality, the hub diameter had been increased to 190 mm on both wheels.

In place of the plunger rear suspension, which the production Horex models employed at that time, the Imperator prototype featured an entirely new and bang-up-to-date full swinging-arm system. This incorporated twin, hydraulically-damped suspension units.

There was no oil tank, as the engine used wet-sump lubrication. A large 20-litre alloy fuel tank,

sponge-rubber saddle, hand-beaten alloy tail fairing, and a chromed exhaust system with short cobby megaphones, rising slightly at the ends, completed the specification.

With only 30 bhp and a claimed 95 mph maximum, the 1951 racing overhead-camshaft Imperator twin was clearly a development prototype, as the factory claimed, rather than a serious racer. Towards the end of that year, the new twin appeared in roadster form. This closely followed the lines of the racer in its basic engineering format, both as regards the power unit and cycle components.

Then it was revealed that the bore and stroke measurements were 65 × 75 mm, giving a capacity of 497 cc. Although commentators at the time expected it to enter full-scale production, in fact, this did not happen (although smaller 392 and 452 cc Imperator roadster twins did appear later). Instead, 1952 saw Horex hard at work on various versions of its best-selling Regina single.

That year also saw the Bad Homburg factory become committed to a full racing programme, with not only the introduction of a revised 500 parallel twin – now with double overhead camshafts – but also new 250 and 350 singles. Although the singles had full works backing, they were the work of the gifted engineer/rider Roland Schnell, who had previously worked wonders with his super-quick Parilla specials.

All three of the new racers made their début at Germany's early-season Dieburger race meeting on 6 April. Interest naturally centred around the half-litre twin, two examples of which were wheeled to the line by Friedl Schön and Hugo Schmitz. As on the Schnell 250/350 singles, the frames closely resembled the trend-setting Norton Featherbed type, except that on the Horex models, the bracing tubes did not cross over near the steering head.

The bottom end of the twin-cylinder engine remained virtually unchanged from the 1951 sohc type, with unit-construction and four-speeds. From the crankcases up, however, the power unit was far removed from the original. Both the alloy cylinders and heads featured vastly increased finning and, of course, the central chain drove twin overhead camshafts. Two valves (although some pundits had suggested four) per cylinder were featured, together with exposed hairpin valve springs. Carburation was taken care of by twin 29 mm Dell'Orto SS1 racing instruments with a single, remote, central float chamber. The carbs themselves were quite steeply inclined at 45 degrees. Ignition was provided by a twin-spark, crankshaft-mounted magneto.

The gifted engineer and rider Roland Schnell. He created 250, 350 and, finally, 500 cc dohc singles for the Horex factory in the period 1952–4

Transmission was taken care of by a clutch which had been modified to a dry type, with a massive air scoop on the offside of the crankcase. Interestingly, although the gearbox was housed within the crankcases, the engine was not of true unit-construction. In fact, the gearbox was contained in a separate, cylindrical casing which was free to rotate within its housing. As its mainshaft was off centre, turning it to a new position provided adjustment of the duplex primary chain.

The cycle parts were largely unchanged from the previous year, except for the frame itself. However, there were subtle improvements.

For example, the forks not only sported rubber gaiters, but also a strong front fork brace/mudguard support, while the rider was provided with an additional pair of footrests, set further to the rear.

These were fitted in such a position on the rear spindle, aft of the rear units, that the pilot could lay almost flat (a scheme pioneered by Guzzi star Fergus Anderson) along the fast straights. In the days before streamlining, this stance was often worth an extra 5 mph to the maximum speed.

As for the smaller bikes, Roland Schnell had certainly waved his magic wand to create a pair of highly interesting Horex 'specials'. However, the 250 and 350 were so alike that the observer needed to inspect the respective model closely to identify exactly which one it was – the only real give-away was the background colour of its racing plates.

The dominant feature of each was the massive casing for the drive chain to the inlet camshaft, which gave them a similar appearance to the works AJS 3-valve model. On the nearside of the camshaft housing, there was a further chain drive to the exhaust cam. Again, there were exposed hairpin valve springs, and two sparking plugs were fitted (one on each side of the head), although quite often

Schnell also introduced Hermann Gablenz to Horex. He is seen here with a 250 single in April 1952

only one was actually employed. Ignition was by a Bosch magneto, and the rev-counter was driven off the exhaust cam.

As with the twin, carburation was via a steeply-inclined Dell'Orto SS1 instrument. An unusual feature was the very extensive finning on the crankcase. This was not an oil container, because the lubrication was dry sump, an alloy tank being fitted below the nose of the racing seat. There was a separate, four-speed, close-ratio gearbox.

The first classic appearance of the new team came at Berne, where the 1952 Swiss GP was staged over the tree-lined 4.5-mile Bremgarten circuit on 18–19 May. Before this, in a non-championship race on Sunday 12 May, at Hockenheim, Friedl Schön had shown what the new double-knocker twin was capable of by taking it to a sensational victory in the Senior race at an average speed of 99.73 mph. Unfortunately, the venture into Switzerland was to be rather different...

The meeting was staged in hot, sunny weather, and there was a large number of works entries, not only from Germany (BMW, DKW and Horex), but also Italy (Moto Guzzi, Gilera, MV and Parilla) and Britain (AJS and Norton). In the 250 race, a Horex, ridden by Hermann Gablenz, came home eighth (and last). On the 350, Schnell himself could finish no higher than 16th out of 20 finishers, and in the 500 cc event, both Horex twins retired ignominiously.

A couple of months later, for the German Grand Prix at the Solitude circuit on 22 July, Horex made a bid for classic honours once more. The Bad Homburg factory even signed up the leading British Continental circus star, Bill Petch, in an attempt to gain honours. However, whilst practising, Petch had a valve drop on the 500 dohc twin and was a non-starter in the race. Even so, he was reported as having been impressed enough to ride the bike later that season. If this was not bad enough, another Horex rider, Kurt Mansfeld, had injured his back after crashing another of the twins in practice.

However, in the 250 race, Horex enjoyed some consolation for these problems when Gablenz took one of the dohc singles to a magnificent third place behind race-winner Felgenheier, on a works DKW twin, and leading Guzzi privateer, Thorn-Prikker.

At the end of the season, persistent rumours concerning the poor performance and reliability of the 500 twin were finally confirmed when it was announced, in October, that the machine was being scrapped. If Horex fielded a twin the following year, it would be completely redesigned, possibly with gear-driven camshafts.

This proved to be accurate information. When the 1953 racing season commenced, although the Schnell singles were virtually unchanged from the 1952 machines, this certainly did not apply to the larger-bore parallel twin. As forecast, the engine had received a considerable amount of extra tuning, although it still retained chain drive to the overhead camshafts.

The gearbox and clutch had been completely redesigned, and repositioned, while the clutch had been transferred to the rear offside of the engine – to the position formerly held by the gearbox. This, in turn, had been fitted in a more conventional position within the centre of the crankcase. The gearchange pedal was now on the offside.

A revised, much smaller, housing was fitted in front of the exposed clutch in place of the crankshaft generator assembly, which had been replaced by a much simpler, total-loss battery/coil system. The carburettors had been mounted on much longer induction manifolds which carried them up to a position almost immediately beneath the seat.

The frame, front forks and wheels remained unchanged, but the rear tail fairing had been deleted. A new seat, deeply-scalloped alloy fuel tank and an alloy fairing assembly had been fitted. Finally, a new exhaust system with shallow-taper megaphones, and rear shocks sporting exposed springs completed the facelift.

Although they took part in the German National Championships, the Horex équipe's main thrust in 1953 was in the classics. These got under way that year in the Isle of Man, but Horex did not join the fray until the second round in Holland. Unfortunately, the Dutch TT at Assen was not to prove a happy hunting ground that year, as not one Horex lasted the distance.

A week later came the Belgian GP over the super-fast Spa Francorchamps circuit. Obviously, the pace did not entirely agree with the Bad Homburg machinery, Fritz Klager's 17th position in the 350 race on one of the Schnell singles being the best result. A couple of weeks after this came the German GP at Schotten. This was destined to be a meeting beset with controversy.

First of all, the majority of foreign riders on works

One of the Schnell-Horex double-knocker singles (a 350) at the 1952 Swiss GP

Engine and gearbox assembly from a 350 Schnell-Horex single, August 1952

machinery refused to take part – on the grounds that the ten-mile circuit was too dangerous for the latest 350 and 500 cc Grand Prix machinery. This came after numerous trees had been felled in the vicinity of the more difficult corners.

Then the status of the 250 cc race was affected when Enrico Lorenzetti fell from his machine while entering the pits during practice and injured his foot; his team-mate, Fergus Anderson, announced that he had no intention of racing. Thus, Montanari rode the only factory Moto Guzzi in the event. German riders, perhaps because of their familiarity with the circuit, expressed no concern about it.

The Schotten track wound through the picturesque Vogel mountains, some 2400 ft above sea level, the road abounding in steep gradients and sinuous turns. It was lined by trees for almost its entire length.

Towards the end of the lap, the road dropped steeply through a series of acute hairpin corners. In the main, the surface was of concrete, and where the concrete sections had broken up, repairs had been carried out with tar. Added to this was a poor safety record, including Geoff Duke's 1952 accident which had ruined his chances of retaining the 500 cc World Championship that year.

With much of the significant competition not

taking part, Klager did well in the opening stages of the 350 race, holding fifth position before finally retiring. In the 250 event, which followed, the other Schnell/Horex double-knocker single ridden by Georg Braun, finished ninth – not a bad result considering that there was a full complement of both NSU and DKW works machinery, plus Montanari's Guzzi.

However, the really outstanding result for Horex came in the Senior race. Here, the factory's new signing, H. P. Müller, riding an enlarged dohc single – not one of the twins – disputed the lead with the works BMW team, headed by Walter Zeller. At the end, Müller was placed third – an excellent début ride on a brand-new bike!

Unfortunately, this taste of glory was somewhat spoilt when the FIM decided that the results of the 350 and 500 cc races would not count towards the world title. Thus, the points won were deleted.

The results gained at Schotten convinced the Horex management to drop the ill-fated twin and concentrate upon the Schnell singles. This proved a wise move, with Schnell and Müller gaining some notable results that season in both the classics and the German National Championships.

Schnell also had a hand in some of the development work on the Horex production roadsters, including a new front fork assembly.

Horex continued its support of the racing programme into 1954, the season getting under way in promising fashion with victory in the 250 race of the Grand Prix of the Saar, run over the famous two-mile 'round-the-houses' St Wendel road circuit. Riding one of the double-knocker singles, Georg Braun averaged 57.6 mph (this should be compared with the 500 cc class in which the winning speed was only 60.6 mph!).

The following week, Fritz Klager scored a superb third place against the cream of the world's riders in the 350 race at Hockenheim. With Müller now a full-time NSU works rider, Klager and Schnell, together with Braun, made up the Horex team.

The machinery comprised the latest dohc singles in 250, 350 and 500 cc engine capacities. The 1954 bikes sported streamlining that was based very closely on the 'bird-beak' type employed by Moto Guzzi on their 1953 works machinery. Like that of

The 500 Horex single ridden by H. P. Müller in the 1953 Swiss GP at Berne

the Mandello team, this was in hand-beaten, polished alloy, the front mudguard and fairing being seen very much as one integral assembly. Some of the machines were equipped with the Schnell-designed front fork assembly, too.

Even better was to come, when later that month, Braun created a minor sensation by finishing second at the 17th international Eifelrennen on his 500 Horex single. The race-winner was Norton works star Ray Amm. Braun also had the satisfaction of coming home in front of the entire BMW works entry.

It was Braun who, at the beginning of July, made more headline news when he débuted a brand-new Horex during practice for the Belgian GP. This was another parallel twin, but one that owed absolutely nothing to the earlier overweight and unreliable examples. Although it was not actually used in the race, because of a minor lubrication fault, none the less, it put up some very respectable lap times.

Designed by the Austrian engineer Ludwig Apfelbeck (later employed by BMW for design work on its car cylinder heads), the impressive-looking newcomer employed a dohc engine which showed clear influence from the latest NSU Rennmax twin. The Horex power unit carried its oil in a massive alloy sump tank, under the engine's crankcase, and was

nearly square with its 60 × 61.6 mm bore and stroke dimensions, which added up to a capacity of 349 cc. Power output was 38 bhp at 9000 rpm.

Drive to the rev-counter was taken from the offside end of the exhaust camshaft. Hairpin valve springs were employed, while the large-diameter valves were in a special material. Fuel was supplied by twin Dell'Orto carbs, and the ignition was taken care of by a Bosch battery/coil system.

The five-speed gearbox was built in unit with the engine, and a dry, multi-plate clutch was employed. Horex had chosen a backbone-type frame, with the engine assembly hanging underneath and no front downtube. The rear portion formed the pivot point for the swinging arm. A pair of leading-link front forks were of a totally new design for the factory.

The cosmetic details were dominated by a fuel tank that was designed very much as a unit with the handlebar fairing and front mudguard, providing the maximum wind-cheating effect.

The new twin's only other classic outing was to be the 1954 German GP at Solitude where, in front of a vast half-million crowd, Georg Braun came home sixth, averaging 80.73 mph for the 24-lap, 99.57-mile

Prototype dohc, 350 cc twin Horex, designed by the Austrian Ludwig Apfelbeck. Although it showed considerable potential, its fate was sealed when the factory pulled out of Grand Prix racing towards the end of 1954

race. As a point of comparison, Klager, on one of the singles, finished way back in 17th place, a lap behind.

Unfortunately, this was to be the last occasion when Horex entered factory machines in a classic race, as by now the company had begun to feel the first effects of the approaching downturn in sales and subsequent wholesale depression and closures within the industry.

After this, it was left to private tuners to fly the Horex flag, which they did with some level of success into the 1960s – several years after the Bad Homburg factory had ceased motorcycle production during the late 1950s.

A notable entrant and tuner of Horex machines was one Friedl Münch (see Chapter 10), who built much of his early reputation with these machines.

7

König – boats to bikes

Early in 1969, Dipl. Ing. Dieter König, managing director and chief engineer of the König company, decided to build a 500 cc-class, solo road-racing motorcycle for Rolf Braun.

Based in West Berlin, the König factory had built up quite a name during the 1960s – but not for motorcycles, for it was a maker of a successful range of multi-cylinder, two-stroke engines for power-boat racing. It was one of these modified production boat engines, a horizontally-opposed, watercooled, four-cylinder two-stroke, that formed the basis of the bike engine.

Despite a lack of experience at the new game, König was not content to start at club, or even national, level, for the new machine first appeared in the West German Grand Prix at Hockenheim on 11 May 1969. Even on paper, the König engine showed

Jerry Lancaster's 680 cc Baldwin König, March 1973

promise. Together with a Manx Norton racing gearbox and clutch, it weighed 55 kg (110 lb) – less than a Norton engine *without* its gearbox. Usable power was available from 7000 rpm, and its peak power of 68 bhp was produced at 9000 rpm.

In effect, the engine comprised a pair of flat-twins, mounted side by side in the common crankcase. The pressed-up, three-bearing, single crankshaft ran across the frame. Bore and stroke measurements of the four cylinders were classic 'stroker', 54 × 54 mm, while each of the Mahle pistons had a single Dykes-type ring. A belt-driven pump circulated water through a small radiator and a reservoir under the engine.

For bike racing, the boat engine had been equipped with a pair of East German BVF carburettors to improve acceleration. Each of these supplied petroil mixture to one pair of 'fore-and-aft' cylinders, which fired at the same time, while induction was controlled by a single disc valve

situated on top of the crankcase. The exhausts from the front and rear pairs of cylinders were siamesed and ran into a massive expansion chamber over the gearbox.

However, the first prototype was very much a development vehicle rather than a pukka racing unit, and Dieter König fully expected to encounter teething problems. His main fear concerned the cooling system, which he considered (correctly) would need a radiator of larger capacity. Essentially, 1969 wore on through a series of problem-solving exercises, rather than any real racing. However, 1970 saw the development process take a giant leap forward with the addition of the Australian Continental circus star, Johnny Dodds, as rider, and New Zealander Kim Newcombe as development engineer.

By the time the König was raced seriously in the Dutch TT at Assen that year, power was up to around 75 bhp and the gearbox was a six-speeder comprising a Norton shell and Austrian Schafleitner internals. A Krober electronic tachometer was fitted,

König works rider and development engineer Kim Newcombe, Hutchinson 100, Brands Hatch, 5 August 1973 – a week before his fatal accident at Silverstone

while a major revision to the breathing arrangements was the use of a pair of high-level expansion chambers.

Although the machine was fitted with an extra-large radiator, it was a non-finisher due to problems which again centred on ineffective cooling. Despite this, the two-stroke four had impressed with its straight-line speed and acceleration. The next move was to fit a smaller radiator and apply more attention to forced airflow. The smaller radiator also permitted a much narrower fairing, which helped the racer's penetration at higher speeds.

A new frame was promised once the engine had been perfected, but for the time being, it remained much as in the original 1969 design. However, the bottom frame rails were omitted and a square-section

The works model used by Newcombe in the 1973 classics. Except for Agostini's MV Agusta, it was the quickest bike on the circuit

swinging arm was used in place of the old round-tube one. Front forks were Ceriani, the rear Girling, and the racing brakes Fontana.

Also in the pipeline was a larger-capacity version, rumoured at the time to be of 800 cc, but with similar external dimensions. This had already been used successfully on the other side of the Atlantic where, in the USA, König-powered midget racing cars were producing a claimed 120 bhp on alcohol. In June 1970, Newcombe stated: 'On petrol, the figure should be around the 90 bhp mark.'

Dodds continued as König's development rider through 1971, prompted not just by the engine's potential, but also by the earlier (and expensive!) failure of the Italian Linto four-stroke twin, which he and other circus riders had purchased. However, during the season, the Australian's only placing within a GP top ten was a tenth at Hockenheim for the 1971 German GP.

Over the following winter, a major redesign took place. For the first time, the original square engine dimensions were dispensed with, to be replaced by

four cylinders with the short stroke of 50 mm and a 56 mm bore, giving 492.6 cc. The crank was redesigned with two main bearings on the drive side, one at the opposite end, and a fourth in the middle. Lubrication was still by petroil (at a ratio of 16:1), and because the mixture was directed straight at the caged-roller big-ends, there was no need for the usual two-stroke slots in the con-rod eyes, providing additional strength. The small-ends were uncaged needle rollers.

Another major change was to the use of a 45 mm twin-choke Solex carburettor, still controlled by a single inlet disc. The drive to this, from the right-hand end of the crankshaft, looked impossibly weak. Not only did the toothed belt have to change direction from the vertical to horizontal, as it circled the pulleys, but the two rollers which effected the change required the belt to twist through 90 degrees each time to offer its smooth side to the rollers. In practice, however, the arrangement proved quite adequate, as did the similarly weak-looking pair of synthetic rubber bands which drove the water impeller.

However, another feature which did cause problems was the exclusive use of chains in the transmission system. The difficulty centred around the fact that it was still only an engine which its constructors had fitted with a gearbox and a clutch from another source. This usually meant the use of not only the secondary drive chain, but also as many as three triplex chains in the primary transmission, a fact which was to prove an embarrassment later.

The revised power unit made its classic début at the 1972 West German GP, staged around the twists and turns of the difficult Nürburgring. By now, Dodds had left the team, to be replaced by Newcombe, who was doing his own riding, and German Ernst Hiller.

The line-up was formidable, with a pair of MV Agustas ridden by World Champion Giacomo Agostini and Alberto Pagani, works Kawasaki triples with Dave Simmonds and the Japanese rider Araoka, together with a factory Swedish Husqvarna ridden by Bo Granath. These were backed up by a host of leading privateers, including Jack Findlay and Billie Nelson.

Amazingly, the race not only proved that Newcombe's winter development had been spot on, but also that his riding talent was something special. The New Zealander was headed only by the pair of super-fast Italian multis and scored a brilliant third place ahead of Simmonds' Kawasaki. Then came Hiller on the *second* König, with the Husky sixth.

More development work meant that the team did not appear at every round, although Newcombe took another third at the Sachsenring, East Germany, behind Agostini and Rod Gould on a Yamaha. This was followed by a fifth at Anderstorp, Sweden, and a tenth in the French GP at Clermont Ferrand. The Swedish result was truly something, as *Motor Cycle News* reported in their 26 July 1972 issue under the headline 'Impressive Kim'. The article reported: 'After the New Zealander had come through to fifth place after being last on the first lap, Newcombe said, "I had to push to the first corner before it would fire, and then the clutch cable broke on the third lap and I was getting into slides on every corner." The machine's performance proved that air vents he had styled into the fairing seemed to have solved previous overheating problems.'

A newcomer, Paul Eickelburg, had joined the team mid-season, gaining a third place in the Yugoslav GP and an eighth at the Dutch TT. He was also responsible for several non-championship Continental internationals in which Königs performed even better.

Typical was the 500 race at Chimay, Belgium, on Sunday 9 July. Here, Kawasaki team leader Dave Simmonds had looked set for victory until the Englishman's engine seized after three laps. Then

Hiller, on another Kawasaki, took over. However, with three laps to go, the slow-starting König rider, Eickelburg, got by to take the flag 35 seconds ahead of Hiller, followed by yet another König rider.

Perhaps the most impressive König performance of 1972, however, was when Eickelburg won the 500 race at an international meeting held over the Hengelo circuit in Holland on 27 August. In the process, he set a new outright lap record for the three-mile course at 91.28 mph – 3 mph faster than the legendary Jarno Saarinen had achieved in the earlier 350 race on his works Yamaha. Dave Simmonds had taken the lead from the start and was pursued by 350 Yamaha-mounted Chas Mortimer. Then, Simmonds had to pitstop to wire up a loose expansion chamber, allowing Mortimer to take over. However, he could not match the speed of Eickelburg, who had made another slow start, but now passed him.

New Zealander Kim Newcombe. The Kiwi not only scored the marque's only solo Grand Prix victory, but also gained the runner-up spot in the 1973 World Championship

It was the sidecar class to which the König four-cylinder, two-stroke engine was best suited. Here is British driver Gerry Boret during the 1973 West German GP

In 1972 a 680 cc version of the König four had also been introduced – while both 500 and 680 units had débuted in sidecar events. Here, both Rolf Steinhausen (with a fifth in France and a fourth in Austria) and the British Boret brothers, Gerry and Nick, (with a brilliant third in the Isle of Man) had proved the potential of the König for sidecar use at the highest level. As 1973 dawned, the König horizontally-opposed four was set to challenge BMW's long supremacy in sidecar Grand Prix racing.

Its use for the sidecar class had both technical and economic attractions. Spares for the BMW Rennsport engine were becoming even more scarce and, therefore, highly expensive, while the machines fetched a price that almost no one could afford. In contrast, the Berlin outboard-based engine units were available at a reasonable price and, perhaps more importantly, with readily-available spares at a fraction of the price being asked for BMW components.

There were problems with the König, too, however. Besides the transmission weakness mentioned earlier, the sidecar constructor also had to cope with the fact that the König had a total lack of engine braking compared to the BMW twin. So an outfit needed powerful brakes – either massive drums or a pair of the discs which were starting to take over from them at the front.

The very first Grand Prix of 1973, staged at Le Castellet, France, saw König machines take honours in both the two- and three-wheel categories. In the solo class, Newcombe gained a fifth at the start of what was to be a year both of sweet success and bitter tragedy.

However, it was the chair-men who really flew the

Berlin company's flag that day, three of the first six outfits home being Königs. Although World Champions Klaus Enders and Ralf Engelhardt kept their works BMW ahead, they were hard-pressed for most of the race by the König pair, Jeff Gawley and Peter Sales. They were ahead of Schwarzel and Kleis on another König, with Steinhausen and Scheurer on yet another coming in fifth.

Gawley showed his form again with a repeat performance behind Enders at the next round, the Austrian GP at the Salzburgring. Following these early successes, many observers were tipping him as a future world champion. However, the lack of funds and mechanical problems meant that his championship thrust was all but over, his only other top-six placing being another second, this time in Belgium mid-season. The Englishman finally finished fifth in the world series.

Another König pair, however, came through to second in the world series. This was the team of Schwarzel and Kleis who, besides their fifth in the opener in France, scored in almost every round, the highlight of which was a second place at Hockenheim. Although König did not win a single sidecar GP, yet another second from the Boret brothers in Holland (their only GP finish that year) meant that

Below
Rolf Steinhausen and passenger Werner Kapp during the 1973 500 cc Sidecar TT

Jeff Gawley's König at the 1973 TT. After showing great potential in the early rounds, his championship effort faded through lack of finance

the flat-four 'strokers' had mounted a serious challenge to BMW's supremacy.

Confirming this were the speed-trap figures carried out during the IoM TT, when the fastest 500 sidecar was the Boret's König at 130 mph, while in the 750 class Gawley's 680 König was fastest, screaming through the electronic eye at 136 mph. This was a record for the chairs, beating the previous best of 134.8 mph, set by Helmut Fath with his four-cylinder 500 Münch URS in 1969.

In the solo class, 1973 saw the König reach its development peak, one man achieving world-class results. This was Kim Newcombe, who not only scored the marque's only solo Grand Prix victory, but also gained the runner-up position in the World Championships, splitting the MV Agusta pair of Phil Read and Giacomo Agostini in the process. However, this excellent result was to end in disaster when the New Zealander was tragically killed on 12 August while competing at Silverstone, with only one round left to go at Jarama in Spain.

Following his fifth in the season's opener in France, Newcombe had taken a third in Austria, victory in Yugoslavia, second in Holland, fourth in Belgium, third in Sweden and, finally, fourth in Finland. However, it was his Yugoslavian win at the Opatija circuit on 17 June which created the headlines; 'Newcombe takes the lead with first Grand Prix win', as *Motor Cycle News* reported it. Newcombe summed it up like this: 'I just can't believe I have won. We have been trying for so long to get the König over the line first and now all the effort seems worthwile.'

Following the New Zealander's death, much of the momentum seemed to go out of König's race effort — certainly in the solo class where there were virtually no successes on two wheels in 1974. History records that a König finished fourth in the 500 West German GP at the Nürburgring that year, but this was an empty result, as there were only *four* finishers after the race was spoilt by a mass withdrawal of star riders on safety grounds.

On three wheels, however, it was to prove a totally different story, with Königs scoring three classic victories and securing second (Schwarzel) and fifth (Steinhausen) in the title chase. Added to this were four seconds, including George O'Dell and Barry Boldison's runner-up spot in the IoM TT, so that it soon became apparent that Königs had real championship potential for 1975.

The chances of this had been greatly reinforced by two factors. The first was the engine's greatly enhanced reliability; the second was the withdrawal of König's major competitor. Many had said that the 1974 championship had only been retained for

BMW by the highly-skilled riding of the victors, Klaus Enders and passenger Ralf Engelhardt, taking their sixth and fifth world titles respectively. Accustomed to winning easily, that year they had seen ever-increasing competition from König, which kept the title in dispute until the very last round. It may have been this which influenced the BMW team's decision to retire at the end of the season.

Enders' sponsor and tuner, Dieter Büsch, transferred his allegiance to Steinhausen and König for 1975, and this faith was repaid in full when Steinhausen and Josef Huber took the World Championship on the Büsch/König by winning three of the seven rounds staged. (An eighth, scheduled for Imola, in Italy, was not run due to organizational problems.)

In fact, except for the domestic West German event, which Rolf Biland won on a Yamaha, every round went to a König; Schwarzel and Huber won two rounds, and Schmidt and Matile another. As a result, König also took second and fourth places in the championship that year.

At the start of the 1975 season, the success of the König engine had prompted the Austrian gearbox specialist, Michael Schafleitner, to build a batch of 20 special six-speed gear clusters for use in König-powered sidecar outfits. He commented at the time: 'A closer set of ratios are needed than any of my previous designs, to make full use of the König's power output.' This was true, as although the solo König could make use of power from as low as 4–5000 rpm, the extra demands (and weight) of a racing sidecar outfit greatly reduced this ability so that the engine had to be kept spinning above 8000 rpm to produce its maximum output and torque. The Büsch-tuned König was rumoured to produce well over 90 bhp – substantially up on the 1975–6 production racing engine, which turned out a claimed 85 bhp at 10,000 rpm.

1975 was the final year in which works-supported Königs were raced in the solo class. Early in the year, Frenchman Christian Leon, dropped by the French Kawasaki team, signed up to race the Königs used by the late Kim Newcombe. In February, he had tested both 500 and 680 Königs at the Paul Ricard circuit and was reported to have been very impressed. On standard engines, he got round in 1 minute, 15.6 seconds, four-fifths of a second outside the lap record held by the late Jarno Saarinen. Leon had two 500s, plus two spare engines, and one 680, plus a spare engine. The 1975 version of the solo 500 had the engine tuned to allow the exhaust system to run under the seat, while the 680 sported magnesium wheels, triple Brembo discs and Marzocchi front forks.

In 1975 Rolf Steinhausen (far right) became König's first world champion. He talks here with the leading British driver Mac Hobson (second left) in September that year

The Leon deal was part of what was termed, at the time, 'a major factory effort'. Other Königs were scheduled to be raced in solo events that year by Horst Lahfield, former West German Junior Champion, but in the World Championships, the team was dogged by a series of retirements. Only three finishes in the top ten were made all season, with Lahfield taking a fine fifth at the Salzburgring in the Austrian GP and a sixth in the Finnish GP at Imatra. Leon's only placing was a seventh at Hockenheim.

In 1976, the solo effort was over. However, Steinhausen retained his world title, with victories in Austria, the Isle of Man and Belgium, while Schwarzel won at the Nürburgring. Many other excellent results were also gained by König-powered outfits at all levels, from club events to Grands Prix.

This reign at the top, however, was to be very brief, for other, more suitable, engines were starting to appear – notably from Yamaha and Fath. Both of these power units featured an integral gearbox and clutch, something which the König never had. Thus, 1977 witnessed all of König's top contenders for championship honours defecting to other engines.

Steinhausen now had a Büsch-tuned Yamaha, while Schwarzel went with ARO-Fath power. The result was inevitable, and except for the previously unknown partnership of Venus and Bittermann, who took a fine second place at Hockenheim, the highest-placed outfit in the 1977 world series was Steinhausen's Büsch-König at the same event, before the team switched to Yamaha power. The challenge from the tiny Berlin factory was over.

A few 680 Königs were raced solo at private level, and two of these were British efforts. One was the Crossier Special, ridden by Scotsman Bob Steel, while the other was owned by Roy Baldwin and ridden by Jerry Lancaster.

From 1977 on, however, virtually nothing was heard of König, the remaining machinery (both solo and sidecar) disappearing from the scene very quickly. Even though König was at the top for a few years only, none the less, it scored some excellent results at the highest level in the mid 1970s. Consequently, it has earned a permanent place in the history of motorcycle road racing, even though it never built a roadster or ventured into other branches of the sport.

Rolf Steinhausen/Wolfgang Kallaugh (500 Büsch-König) at Ramsey Hairpin during their successful drive to second place in the 1977 Sidecar TT

8
Kreidler – tiddler champions

Originally formed shortly after World War 2 by Alfred Kreidler as a specialist supplier of non-ferrous tubing, sheet and wire, Kreidler GmbH decided to enter the ranks of motorcycle manufacturing in 1951. The company's production facilities were situated at Kornwestheim, just to the north of the great city of Stuttgart, capital of the State of Baden-Wurtemburg and the largest and one of the most beautiful cities of south-western Germany.

Dr Kreidler's diversification centred around the design and manufacture of a 49 cc moped, the K50. Built for reliability, the 38 × 44 mm bore and stroke, piston-ported two-stroke soon became a firm favourite, and sales reflected this by rocketing Kreidler to the top of West Germany's booming ultra-lightweight market. Cheap and easy to run, the K50 attracted many a youngster to motorcycling,

Moped racer – Kreidler's first racer of 1960 was exactly that, a stripped and tuned Florett roadster

and it was only a matter of time before the first Kreidler was put to competitive use. This came in late 1958, initially off-road, but soon afterwards in road racing, as the first ranks of 50 cc tarmac racers began to appear in the Fatherland.

Essentially, a group of enthusiasts at the Kornwestheim works decided to build a machine based on the recently-introduced Florett (Foil). However, even for this first prototype, there was an air of official backing, as the project had to be authorized by the autocratic Dr Kreidler.

In reality, this first racer was a standard Florett, with pressed-steel frame, Earles-type front forks, a mildly-tuned engine and a set of specially-made, close-ratio gears. Even the fan cooling of the Florett was retained, together with the road-going silencer. The Kreidler was the quietest, if not the quickest, machine in the race! Even so, it was surprisingly successful, which prompted Dr Kreidler to take a more serious interest. The result was victory in the

Above
*Hans-Georg Anscheidt rode this much more purposeful
Kreidler in 1961 to win the Coupe d'Europe title. He is
shown here during the Hockenheim round*

Below
*The 1961 works Kreidler engine looked like this. Note
rotary-valve induction, two Dell'Orto carbs and
comprehensive finning for head and barrel – 8 bhp at
11,000 rpm*

1960 West German 50 cc Racing Championship
series.

For 1961, the sport's organizing body, the FIM,
decided to put 50 cc racing on a firmer footing by
instigating the Coupe d'Europe. In effect, this was a
series of international races with a minimum duration requirement, run on rules which normally
applied to the full Grand Prix events.

A total of eight race organizers staged Coupe
d'Europe events during 1961 – three in Belgium, two
in Germany and one each in Holland, Spain and
Yugoslavia. Rather surprisingly, neither Italy nor
Britain showed much interest, although the tiddlers
had been popular in both countries for several years.

Although Kreidler did not contest all the rounds,
it still came out victorious. This was due, in no small
part, to the superb riding of one of its employees,
Hans-Georg Anscheidt.

Born in East Prussia, at Konisberg, in 1935,
Anscheidt had started his motorcycling career in off-
road competitions during 1953. With the urge to go
faster, he switched to grass, cinder and sand races.
Between 1957 and 1959, he won a total of 21 races
out of the 40 he entered.

Shortly afterwards, he became a works rider when
he took his Kreidler to a gold medal in the 1960
ISDT, while being employed in the factory's testing
and development department. It was also in 1960
that he became a road racer and subsequently won
the Hockenheim Motor Cup for his factory.

Although still based on the production Florett

A jubilant Hans-Georg Anscheidt with victor's laurels after being proclaimed FIM Coupe d'Europe in 1961

engine, the 1961 Coupe d'Europe winning machine had been modified to rotary-valve induction halfway through the season. It also featured twin Dell'Orto carburettors and a six-speed gearbox. With a claimed power output of 8 bhp, the ultralightweight flyer was capable of around 80 mph.

The machine upon which Anscheidt's Renn (racing) Florett was based continued to sell in ever-increasing numbers. By 1962, an astonishing 50 per cent of all powered two-wheelers sold in Germany were of Kreidler manufacture.

On this basis, one could be forgiven for thinking that the Kornwestheim plant would have sported a lavish competitions department. However, this was not the case. The development team, led by Dipl. Ing. Johannes Hilber (who had joined Kreidler from the aircraft industry), all worked in the standard production research and development office and returned there each Monday morning. Not only this, but all the riders, including Anscheidt, were recruited from the factory's staff. At that time, it was an unwritten rule that you had to work for the company to get a works ride!

For 1962, the FIM introduced a full-blown 50 cc World Championship series. In response to this, Kreidler set to and came up with a much improved machine to challenge the world.

Even before this, Kreidler realized that the conventional piston-ported, racing two-stroke, developed from the Florett roadster, was about at the end of its power line. Thus, in June 1961, during the later stages of the Coupe d'Europe, they had begun racing with a rotary-valve engine. Development continued through the winter months, with the result that the factory was ready to meet the Japanese onslaught when the first of the 1962 classics took place around the twists and turns of Montjuich Park, Barcelona, the scene of the Spanish GP in April 1962.

Like the Florett-based engine, the full GP unit employed a horizontal layout, the head pointing forward. To gain the maximum possible capacity, Hilber's team used a bore of 40 mm and a stroke of 39.7 mm to give 49.9 cc. Amazingly, the crankshaft was taken directly from the production roadster, which spoke well of the reliability and engineering of Kreidler products. A special Mahle piston was used.

The cylinder barrel was cast in aluminium and finished with a 'pin-pricked' hard-chrome running surface. The idea was that the tiny holes would retain oil for improved lubrication, so important to a seizure-prone two-stroke.

In fact, Kreidler was the first German motorcycle manufacturer to use this system, which had been developed by Porsche for their high-performance cars. It should also be noted that another German marque, TWN (Triumph), had pioneered the chrome-plated cylinder bore on its production two-strokes in the immediate post-war period. There was also the use of magnesium for the outer engine covers.

For carburettors, Kreidler abandoned the Italian Dell'Ortos used in 1961 and fitted a pair of special Bings (one for each rotary valve) made to their specifications. The cost of these carbs was as much as the normal Florett sports moped!

The power was routed through a 12-speed gearbox. Actually, there were only four speeds, the other ratios being obtained by means of an external, three-speed overdrive controlled by a twistgrip on the handlebars. Even Hilber thought this excessive, but opted for it because the effective power only existed between 9500 and 11,000 rpm. For certain national events, however, including the German hill-climb championships, only eight ratios were used, simply because of the more-or-less constant gradients. The

Much of the 1961–2 closed season was spent on developing the optimum fairing in a Stuttgart wind tunnel

12 ratios were intended solely for pukka Grand Prix action, not shorter courses.

Of course, the real problem with a highly-strung 50 cc racing motorcycle was insufficient torque. As the power output and engine revolutions crept up, so this became even more apparent. Naturally, the Kreidler men did not use all 12 gears for each corner, nor even half of them, but they had enough gears to allow the right one to be selected for every corner on the circuit. Changing up was not a problem, the trick, according to Anscheidt, was 'remembering where you started on the down-changes.'

The 1962 racing Kreidler frame was manufactured from aircraft-quality, chrome-moly tubing. Unlike the 1961 version, this had a sort of parallel oval design, in which the two main tubes were one continuous unit each, running from the steering head down and back to support the engine, and around and up to the steering head once more. They were cross-braced, not quite half-way back. A triangular pressing of steel was fitted at the rear of

this twin-hoop system, furnishing the main engine mounting point, the swinging-arm pivot and a platform for the 6-volt, 7-amp/hour battery.

The Earles-type front fork used adjustable spring lugs, as they had done in the previous year. Experience with racing these tiny machines had shown Kreidler that attention to the suspension system made up for any slight decrease in outright power output compared to a rival who had a faster, but less well-handling motorcycle.

Keeping the bike on the ground was one of the major problems with a dry weight of only 55 kg (118 lb). Riders had to weigh a minimum of 60 kg (132 lb), otherwise ballast had to be fitted to the machine to make up the difference.

The fairing itself was the result of a full winter's work. Using a Stuttgart wind tunnel, Kreidler put Anscheidt in the riding position and went to work, using a mesh fairing that could be covered with flexible plastic and bent in small increments until the most perfect form was found.

Braking was improved for 1962 with larger-diameter front drums. Manufactured from Electron, these weighed no more than the smaller units fitted the previous year. The rear drums remained the same, except that they were now cast, rather than machined from a solid block.

To counter the might of Japan, Dr Kreidler finally waived the rule which forbade non-factory employees from riding his bikes. This allowed the Dutch rider, Jan Huberts, to join the team, which also consisted of Anscheidt, Wolfgang Gedlich and Rudolf Kunz.

The first two championship rounds went to the West German factory, with team leader Anscheidt winning the inaugural Spanish GP, and Huberts taking the flag in France. However, even though the Dutchman won at the Sachsenring in East Germany, and Anscheidt at Monza, ex-MZ star Ernst Degner, riding a Japanese Suzuki, took the title. Anscheidt finally finished the year as runner-up in the championships, while Huberts was fourth.

For 1963, a new duplex chassis, stronger (telescopic) forks and more powerful brakes were provided, together with more power – 12 bhp. Even so, it was still not enough steam to stem the tide of the mighty Japanese. Anscheidt fought tooth-and-nail, right down to the final Grand Prix, but Suzuki and Hugh Anderson won the day, and with it the second 50 cc world title.

Determined to achieve better results in 1964, Kreidler pulled out all the stops and came up with an almost totally new bike. The horizontal engine had seen a considerable amount of development during the winter, with a new, larger-fin cylinder, new expansion-chamber exhaust and beefier aircooled clutch. Its 12 gears had been changed to six in the engine, with a two-speed, cable-operated overdrive. The new chassis was a notable improvement, and it held the now 100 mph, 14 bhp motor under a lattice-work of tubing, while up front, a pair of 30 mm, leading-axle telescopic forks were fitted with an Electron, 170 mm (7 in), single-leading-shoe, drum front brake. Narrow and extremely light, the new Renn Florett, with rider Anscheidt, was ready to cross swords with the Japanese.

The season began with a fourth in the United States Grand Prix at Daytona raceway. Following hot

The first round of the newly-introduced 50 cc World Championship series was staged at Montjuich Park, Barcelona, in May 1962. Here, Kreidler riders Anscheidt (18) and Huberts (15) lead local Derbi ace, Busquets. Anscheidt won the event

on the heels of the Stateside event came a great result in Barcelona, where Anscheidt put it across the Japanese in no uncertain fashion to score a memorable victory. Unfortunately, this early promise could not be sustained and, yet again, Suzuki and Hugh Anderson took the 1964 50 cc World Championship with the Japanese marque's latest featherweight racer, the rear-exhaust RM64.

For 1965, Kreidler stuck with very much the same machine as the previous year – with its horizontal, rotary-valve induction, single-cylinder motor and some 14 bhp of puff. But it should have all been so different . . .

In 1963, a 50 twin had been designed, but not built because of disagreement at boardroom level. Had that engine been authorized, it could well have been the leading entry in its class. As it was, Dr Kreidler finally gave the go-ahead in early 1965, but by then it was too late. The Japanese had dropped their development into overdrive and simply blew the much smaller German company into the weeds, with machines such as the twin-cylinder RK65 Suzuki and Honda's jewel-like RC114 dohc twin. The best Anscheidt and Kreidler could do all year was a fourth place in the final round in Japan.

This finally sealed the fate for Kreidler, and its autocratic boss pulled the plug on the GP effort. The result was that Anscheidt upped and left, signing almost immediately for Suzuki, for whom he became thrice World Champion in 1966, 1967 and 1968. Furthermore, the long-awaited twin never made it to a Grand Prix start line.

Another blow to the Kornwestheim factory's pride fell in May 1965, when its German rival, Zündapp, snatched Kreidler's 50 cc speed records at Monza.

However, that particular acid drop was not savoured for long. Soon, Dr Kreidler sent his men into action to reclaim this honour, and several others, at the Bonneville Salt Flats, Utah, in October that year.

The rider for these record attempts was Rudolf Kunz. It was Kunz who had the honour of establishing the very first world record for the standing-start quarter mile, when his streamlined Kreidler clocked a mean time of 19.586 seconds, giving an average speed of 45.96 mph.

The 1965 Spring Congress of the FIM in Moscow had agreed to recognize standing quarter records from 31 May onward. At the same time, the mile, both for standing and flying starts, was reinstated as a record distance after a lapse of nearly nine years.

Kunz also took the standing-start mile record with

Above
British journalist David Dixon tested Anscheidt's works Kreidler after the 1963 TT. Here, he proved that it was truly ultra-lightweight

Overleaf
Anscheidt on his way to victory in the Hutchinson 100 at Silverstone, 1965. By now, the engine was giving 14 bhp. Other changes included a new frame and telescopic front forks to replace the original Earles type

a mean time of 53.506 seconds (67.28 mph), handsomely beating Massimo Pasolini's 1956 Aermacchi average of 51.5 mph.

Kreidler's main goal was the 50 cc land speed record, and in the specially prepared, streamlined projectile, Kunz sped through the electronic eye

Above
In 1967 Kreidler offered a race kit for the latest version of the Florett roadster

Below
Rudi Kunz streaks past a group of spectators on his factory Kreidler during the 1970 Ulster Grand Prix at Dundrod

with a two-way average speed of 131.25 mph to claim a new record for the German factory. The bike had a modified 12-speed GP engine, with an electric shift mechanism, that used special fuel and was cooled by ice.

During this period of uncertainty on the competitions front, Kreidler had been going from strength to strength in the sales of its standard production machines. By the mid 1960s, it had captured over 60 per cent of powered two-wheeler sales in Germany and neighbouring Switzerland. The company was doing almost as well in the Netherlands. So although the racing boys were far from happy, the reverse was true in the showroom.

At the Cologne Show in September 1967, Kreidler announced a new dual-purpose 50 cc model, the Florett RS. The single-cylinder, piston-ported two-stroke was basically a roadster, but was sold with a special kit that converted the five-speeder into a fully-fledged racer.

The Kornwestheim factory claimed 5.3 bhp for the RS in roadster trim, the race kit boosting the power output to over 9 bhp, while maximum speed was up to around 80 mph.

The kit comprised a new cylinder, piston and head, Dell'Orto SS1 remote-float racing carburettor,

Kreidler's first world title came in 1971 thanks to the Dutchman Jan de Vries. He is seen here during the Austrian GP that year on his Van Veen-tuned machine

a new induction stub, gaskets, cables, an air lever, racing spark plug, 14- and 15-teeth gearbox sprockets, and a full expansion-chamber exhaust system.

Several private tuners, both in Germany and abroad, soon found ways of making the roadster-based engine even more potent. In the late 1960s, these Kreidlers took over from the Honda CR110 production racer in club and national status events.

One of the first such machines was constructed by Anton Mohr of Koblenz. Whereas the factory obtained around 9.5 bhp from its race-kitted Florett RS engine, Mohr, using modified roadster components, managed to squeeze 14 bhp from his.

Later still, the Dutch-based Van Veen concern produced a cylinder which bumped this figure to over 16 bhp. However, with the engine revving to over 16,000 rpm, unreliability began to rear its ugly head.

As a sign of spiralling costs which the would-be 50 cc private racer had to face for this extra perfor-

mance, the cost of the Van Veen cylinder often exceeded the total cost of a complete factory race-kitted Florett engine unit! However, riders still coughed up for the most competitive bike outside Grand Prix racing.

In 1969, the FIM had restricted 50 cc GP machines to only one cylinder and a maximum of six speeds. This move prompted Kreidler back into action for another shot at that elusive world championship title. However, over the preceding years, development had stagnated and the factory (via its Dutch importers, Van Veen) rejoined the fray with a 15 bhp engine, which was still based around the 1965 rotary-valve, aircooled unit.

Unfortunately for the Kreidler effort, it had reckoned without the Spanish Derbi team which had been slowly developing its single and had a superb, watercooled, disc-valve machine ready for its leading rider, Angel Nieto, to use to claim his first world title. This the pairing followed up with a second in the following year.

Starting with a clean sheet of paper, Van Veen came up with a brand-new Kreidler Grand Prix racer for 1971, developed by the West German two-stroke wizard, Jorg Moller. This effort was financed by the vast sales being enjoyed by Kreidler, not only at home, but in the Netherlands – the 100,000th machine for sale in that country had been produced the same year.

The new GP racer not only featured a totally-revised watercooled engine, producing 17.5 bhp, but also an entirely-new chassis with Italian Ceriani suspension and Fontana drum brakes, the last being a double-sided device at the front.

So dramatic was this advance in development that the metallic-green flyer caught champions Angel Nieto and Derbi completely flat-footed.

Kreidler's leading rider in 1971 was the diminutive Dutchman, Jan de Vries, although occasional rides were given to the likes of Barry Sheene and Jarno Saarinen. With Derbi also drafting in Gilberto Parlotti, the 1971 50 cc title hunt made excellent entertainment.

However, except for Sheene's win in the Yugoslav round, the championship contest was between only two men, Nieto and De Vries.

With five victories in Austria, West Germany,

Van Veen/Kreidler power egg, as used by de Vries to lift the 1971 50 cc World Championship crown

Belgium, Italy and Spain, compared to Nieto's three, De Vries finally put Kreidler's name on the World Championship trophy.

However, the Amsterdam-based Van Veen/Kreidler team did not have it all its own way in the following year, for Derbi and Nieto responded to their defeat by coming up with an improved machine for 1972. Jan de Vries and the Spaniard were neck-and-neck all season, with the Dutch rider slightly ahead going into the final round – in Spain!

On home territory and spurred on by the fanatically partisan crowd, Nieto crossed the line at the front of the field. This result produced a dead-heat in the title race, for both riders had scored an identical number of points and each had won three races.

No title hunt had ever been this close before, so the FIM decided to take the five Grand Prix races in which both riders had finished and add up the total times. This gave Nieto the championship by only 21.32 seconds. The actual totals were: Nieto, 2 hours, 27 minutes, 26.29 seconds; de Vries, 2 hours, 27 minutes, 47.61 seconds.

Derbi announced its retirement from Grand Prix racing at the end of 1972, and the following year,

Below

The Van Veen/Kreidler employed an Italian front end in 1971 – Fontana double-sided front brake and Marzocchi forks

Above

The 1971 Van Veen team bikes ridden by Jan de Vries (foreground) and Jos Schurgers. The cylinders were different – de Vries' was square, Schurgers' was round

Kreidler took the championship and four of the top five placings; Jan de Vries was World Champion with Kreidler for the second time in three seasons.

In 1974, Henk van Kessel took the title for the West German marque. To prove how total the Kreidler dominance had become, the top six riders were mounted on the Kornwestheim factory's machinery.

In an attempt to get his championship back, Angel Nieto joined Kreidler for the 1975 season. He made the right choice, too, taking the title with victories at six of the eight rounds staged that year.

Nieto had chosen Kreidler for the simple reason that, at the time, it was the best machine by a huge margin. The ultra-professional Van Veen organization had swept the opposition aside in a most convincing fashion.

It was because of this fact that the Spanish Motorcycle Federation (who effectively controlled the sport in that country) sanctioned Nieto to ride a foreign bike. At that time, the country was still under the rule of the dictator Franco, which usually meant that a Spanish rider could not race anything built outside the frontiers of Spain.

The reason Nieto wanted the chance to ride a Kreidler is amply illustrated by the fact that, during the 1974 Belgian GP, Van Kessel's machine had lapped at an amazing 101.7 mph. With the power output now raised to over 19 bhp, this gave the latest Kreidler a maximum speed in excess of 125 mph!

Although the basic running gear, such as the spine-type frame, Ceriani forks and Fontana drum brakes remained unchanged, development of the watercooled, rotary-disc-induction engine had been untiring, with the constant search for not only extra horsepower, but also improved engine torque. The last was of vital importance following the six-speed maximum ruling.

After winning the 1975 title on the Kreidler, Nieto defected to his home camp in 1976, to ride a Bultaco (actually an Italian Piovaticci with Bultaco decals!).

The Spanish team had two aces — not only the undoubted brilliance of Nieto's riding, but the Piovaticci, which was a fully-developed GP contender. It had finished second in the 1975 title chase, ridden by Eugenio Lazzarini, before the team ran into financial difficulties and was snapped up by Bultaco, who wished to make a return to road racing.

Thus, Bultaco and Nieto took the 1976 world title, and retained it in 1977. However, Kreidler came back in 1978 with the former Piovaticci pilot, Lazzarini.

Thereafter, Kreidler followed with a succession of GP victories and world championship titles until the

Above
West German GP, Nürburgring, 30 April 1972. Ludwig Fabbender (Kreidler, 39), Angel Nieto (Derbi, 28) and Jan Bruins (Kreidler, 6) lead the pack into the first turn

Below
Jan de Vries gained his and Kreidler's second title in 1973. He is seen that year on his way to victory in the Belgian GP over the super-fast Spa circuit

Above
Contrary to popular belief, van Kessel's 1974 championship bike was not backed by Van Veen, but was a stock Van Veen/Kreidler production racer, tuned by Jorg Moller. He is shown here in winning form at Imola

Below
The 1974 50 cc World Champion, Henk van Kessel

demise of the 50 cc class at the end of the 1984 season. In 1983 and 1984, the Austrian Stefan Dörflinger won on Krauser machines which, in fact, were Kreidlers under a different name, following the collapse of the Kornwestheim factory during 1982. These last bikes were tuned by Herbert Rittberger and developed 21 bhp from the 41.5×36 mm, six-transfer-port engine.

Before this sad finale, a production version of the Van Veen/Kreidler GP racer had taken its bow early in 1978. This was developed by the same Jorg Moller who had been instrumental in the original Van Veen design.

With a power output of 16.5 bhp at 16,000 rpm, the production racer was very similar to the mid-1970s works bike. It was a match for anything outside GP racing in the 50 cc class.

Fitted with 18 in. cast-alloy wheels and front and rear hydraulically-operated disc brakes (of 210 and 190 mm diameter respectively), the watercooled, rotary-disc-valve machine sported the 40×39.7 mm Kreidler bore and stroke measurements, which could be traced all the way back to the production roadsters of the 1950s. In reality, however, this was about all these machines had in common.

The Mahle piston and Nickasil bore had an operating clearance of micro-millimetres, and because of this, there were 15 piston sizes, each to suit a particular piston/cylinder measurement. As

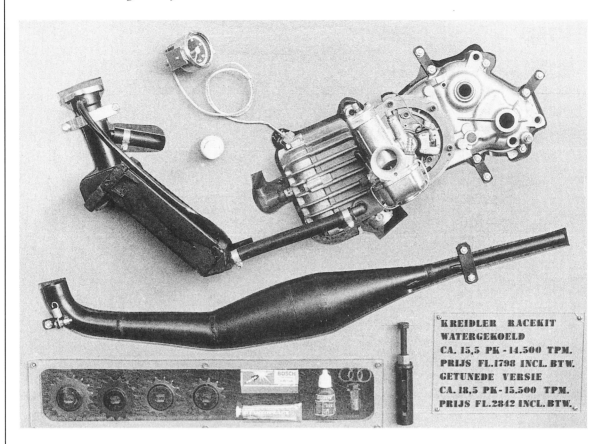

KREIDLER RACEKIT
WATERGEKOELD
CA. 15,5 PK - 14.500 TPM.
PRIJS FL.1798 INCL. BTW.
GETUNEDE VERSIE
CA. 18,5 PK - 15.500 TPM.
PRIJS FL.2842 INCL. BTW.

Above
Amsterdam Show, 1974, and the Van Veen/Kreidler race kit for sale to well-off privateers

with the works machines of the period, the production racer employed Krober capacity-discharge ignition, the trigger of which was mounted on a solid bronze outer disc housing. The 28 mm Bing carburettor was normally ditched in favour of the superior 29 mm Mikuni instrument, which could be obtained cheaply by boring out a standard production carburettor from one of the aircooled RD250/400 Yamaha roadster twins.

When Stefan Dörflinger had piloted his Krauser/Kreidler to the 1983 50 cc world crown, it had raised the factory's total to seven championships, a record that looks secure as the FIM has now abandoned the class. It is a fitting tribute to the marque which can truly claim to have been 'King of the tiddlers'.

Left
Spanish flyweight racing star Angel Nieto joined Kreidler in 1975. He made the right choice, too, taking the 50 cc title with victories at six out of the eight rounds staged that year

Below
Production version of Van Veen/Kreidler GP bike of the late 1970s. Producing 16.5 bhp at 16,000 rpm, it was a match for anything except a full works entry

Above
Nieto (10) challenges another Kreidler rider for the lead in his championship year on the German tiddler

9

Maico – from dirt to tarmac

The history of Maico is very much one of the Maisch family and can be traced back to the year 1926 with the formation of Ulrich Maisch & Co., in Poltringen, near Stuttgart. However, it was to be another five years – in 1931 – before the first involvement with two-wheelers came about. Then the two young sons of the founder began bicycle manufacture in a small workshop at the rear of the plant, employing a combination of bought-in components and their own work.

The success of the bicycle enterprise led the brothers, Otto and Wilhelm Maisch, to consider manufacturing their own motorcycles. Not only did this lead to their first real bike, the 1935 MP120, an

ultra-lightweight using a 118 cc Ilo single-cylinder, two-stroke engine, but the adoption of the Maico trade name – a contraction of Maisch & Co.

Until 1939, all Maicos employed Ilo power units, but on the very eve of World War 2, an autocycle appeared with a 50 cc Sachs engine.

Additionally, the success of the Maico line had allowed the brothers not only to expand into new and larger premises at nearby Pfaffingen, but also to lay down plans for a new machine incorporating their own ideas. These included the very first engine assembly to be designed and built by Maico itself.

However, with the outbreak of war, Maico found itself manufacturing not the new two-wheeler, but spare parts for the *Luftwaffe* (the German air force).

Thus, the brothers' dream of producing their first all-Maico motorcycle was set back a whole decade. Production of the machine, the M150, did not begin until 1949. Even then, much of this came about by luck – unlike many of Germany's pre-war marques, Maico had escaped both the bombing and the results of being under the control of the Russians, the fate which had befallen DKW, for example.

During the 1950s, Maico steadily built up its business which, by the end of the decade, had become linked with luxury scooters and off-road sport – such as motocross and long-distance trials. Because of this, the company escaped the majority of problems which beset their larger, and more well-known, counterparts within the German motorcycle industry.

Maico continued this niche-type marketing strategy into the 1960s with considerable success,

Prototype 125 Maico production racing engine, March 1968

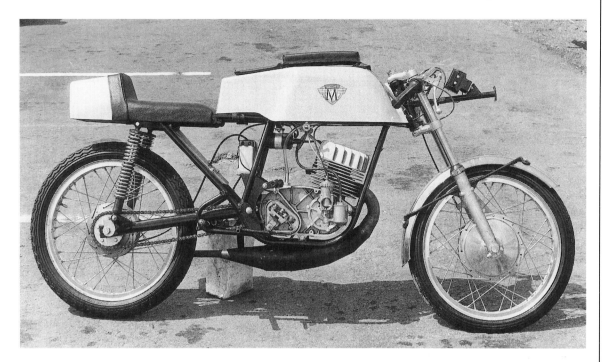

Production 125 Maico RS, as it looked when it was first offered for sale in 1969. Specification included 26–8 bhp, disc-valve induction and six-speed box

but without any real involvement with either roadsters or road racers.

In 1963, however, all this was set to change, for Maico realized that it would have to respond to falling sales of its scooters by designing brand-new street motorcycles to meet a growing demand for high-performance ultra-lightweights.

The answer was two machines, the MD50 and 125, both featuring a totally-new, rotary-valve, five-speed unit-construction engine. These were fast and modern, and they were to play an important role in launching the company back on to the tarmac – both on street and track.

The next stage in the Maico racing story came in September 1966 when it was revealed that Maico would be taking part in European road-racing events the following year. They were to enter works machines for the 125, 250 and 350 classes.

Heading this programme was Dipl. Ing. Günther Schier, who had joined Maico three months before as chief engineer in the construction department, mainly to get the racing machines under way and keep them going. One of Europe's top two-stroke men, Schier was full of enthusiasm for the project and was at the Nürburgring to see Toni Gruber finish a brilliant second in the 350 cc German championship race on a 252 cc (68 × 70 mm) Maico.

Already down to ride 250s and 350s were three top names in German national racing at that time: Günther Fischer, Dieter Braun and Gruber.

The prototype 252 cc machine was powered by a tuned version of the existing motocross engine which, in turn, was based on the Blizzard roadster design of the mid 1950s. This had been designed by Dipl. Ing. Ulrich Pohl, who had left to work for BMW.

During 1967, the Maicos were used with some degree of success in German racing, notably the overbored engine used in the 350 class. The best results were obtained by future World Champion, Dieter Braun. However, the 125 was the machine that showed the most promise. This employed an engine based on the production roadster MD125 unit.

At the 1966 Cologne Show, the MD125 Sport had been launched. With a tuned engine, it gave 14 bhp at 6900 rpm. It was this that was used as a basis for the pukka racing model.

Not only did Maico themselves build prototype 125 racers during the period 1967–8, but also the leading private tuner, Anton Mohr. His machine employed the roadster's bottom end and five-speed gearbox, but with a one-off alloy head and cylinder barrel, the latter with a rearward-facing exhaust port. Other special components included the racing Dell'Orto carb, Oldani front brake and comprehensive, high-level, expansion-chamber exhaust system.

The factory prototypes were similar, but differed in details, such as brakes, carburettor, engine tuning and exhaust. They also had a conventional, front-facing exhaust port.

There were also a low-level expansion chamber, Ceriani forks and Maico's own 2LS, 180 mm front stopper. The 123.67 cc (54 × 54 mm) engine shared the same square dimensions of the roadster, but running on a compression ratio of 15:1 gave a claimed 21 bhp at 11,500 rpm. As on the roadster, the 32 mm Bing carburettor was bolted directly to the crankcase. The gearbox had six close ratios: 1st, 3.07; 2nd, 2.35; 3rd, 1.85; 4th, 1.59; 5th, 1.41; and 6th, 1.32. The dry weight, including streamlining, was a mere 68 kg (150 lb), and the maximum speed, 115 mph.

First production versions of the over-the-counter version, the RS125, made their début at the beginning of the 1969 season. Right from the off, it offered a highly competitive level of performance – witnessed by a fine second place by the Swedish star, Kent Anderson, in the opening round of the 1969 125 cc World Championship at the Spanish GP, held that year at the Jarama circuit.

The same rider repeated this performance to finish second in the Dutch TT at Assen. Coupled to a fourth in Belgium, this gave the Swede – and Maico – fourth overall in the championship table.

Both Anderson and Toni Gruber had received 'works development' machines, rather than standard production bikes, for the 1969 season. This move paid handsome dividends, with not only Anderson's performance in the classics, but Gruber's many excellent results at home.

Even better was to follow. For 1970, Maico signed up another Swedish rider, Borge Jansson, as a replacement for Anderson, who had signed for Yamaha. Gruber provided the back-up again, but this time concentrating on the World Championship series.

The first round was on home ground, over the twists and turns of the Nürburgring, where Gruber came in fourth. Then came the French GP at Le Mans – Jansson showed his potential by finishing an impressive second to Dieter Braun on an ex-works Suzuki twin. Gruber finished fourth in France, then

The interesting and innovative SMZ, which was built by Schlogl, Mang and Zender for Dieter Braun to use in the 250 cc World Championship series, 1972

came the Yugoslav GP at Opatija, where Jansson could finish no higher than fourth.

Next came the long and ultra-demanding Isle of Man TT, where Jansson again displayed his skill, once more finishing second to the combination of Braun and Suzuki.

There followed a series of rather disappointing results before, at the final round in Spain, Jansson rode perhaps his best race of the year to annex third place. He was one place ahead of the new 125 cc World Champion, Dieter Braun, in a race won by local hero Angel Nieto (Derbi), while Barry Sheene (Suzuki) was second.

Jansson's excellent rides that year had earned him third place in the championship, one better than Anderson's a year earlier.

By now, sales of the standard over-the-counter RS125 were beginning to build up nicely, thanks in no small part to the performances gained at world level. To give this an even bigger spur, the factory gained the signature of the 1970 125 cc World Champion, Dieter Braun, for the following season.

Maico engineers responded by carrying out further development work, which raised the power output of the works-supported machines to around 28 bhp at 11,000 rpm. The official team riders comprised Braun, Jansson and Gruber.

At the season's end, Jansson had ridden his Maico

Maico's over-the-counter racer and a grass-tracker powered by a 250 motocross engine exhibited by the British importer, Bryan Goss, during the early 1970s

rotary-valve single to another third place in the championship series. Braun took his to fourth, while the privateer, Bender, scored a very creditable seventh.

All three had scored runner-up positions: Jansson (Isle of Man, Czechoslovakia and Sweden); Braun (Finland); Bender (Belgium).

Development continued into 1972, and Maico was rewarded when Borge Jansson scored its first-ever classic victory, taking the chequered flag in East Germany at the Sachsenring circuit. Jansson's average speed was 96.50 mph. Not content with this, the Swedish rider won the next round at Brno, Czechoslovakia, too! This time he averaged 87.66 mph.

Jansson finished the year as the leading Maico rider yet again, with fourth position overall in the championship table.

Above

Dieter Braun, leading Maico rider and later a champion on Japanese Yamahas

Right

Braun in action with his 125 Maico, West German Grand Prix, 30 April 1972

By now, several privateers were beginning to score championship points, the best result being Bill Rae's excellent third place in the IoM TT that year.

What of Dieter Braun, you may ask? Well, he was becoming more and more involved with the 250 class. For 1972, a trio of his mechanics – Sepp Schlogl, Anton Mang and Alfous Zender – built the highly-interesting and innovative SMZ (coined from the first letters of the three builders' surnames) narrow-angle V-twin.

Both Schlogl and Mang were later to win fame – the former as a leading tuner, the latter as a multi world champion.

Three SMZs were constructed. The first used 125 Maico cylinders and certain other components from

Bill Rae, on his production RS125 single, on his way to an excellent third place during a very wet 1972 125 cc Isle of Man TT

the same source. However, the other two had special cylinders which had been designed by Schlogl and cast by Mahle. Each had five transfer ports and a single exhaust port.

Other notable details included a Mahle crankshaft and pistons, and a six-speed Austrian Schafleitner gearbox. Disc-valve induction and watercooling were also used, the power output of 64 bhp at 12,000 rpm being a highly competitive figure for the era.

In fact, in terms of speed, it was actually faster than the Yamaha works development bikes ridden by the likes of Saarinen and Gould!

Entered as a Maico, the SMZ's weakness was its poor handling. Furthermore, the fact that it was a truly private venture (no help was provided by Maico!) meant that it was at a huge disadvantage compared with its main competitor, Yamaha, and also the Italian Aermacchi marque that year, both of which enjoyed almost unlimited funds.

The best result gained by the SMZ in 1972 was a second behind the Japanese rider Hidi Kanaya at the Nürburgring in the 250 cc West German GP.

Although it had the speed, the team decided to opt for the 'safety' of its own watercooled conversion for the newly-released production TD3 Yamaha for 1973, and it was on this that Braun took the world title that year. Meanwhile, Mang took over the SMZ ride and, in doing so, took his first steps to world fame on his own account.

Before leaving the SMZ saga, it should he said that the machine pointed the way to the future. Indeed, over a decade later, the mighty Honda team and its rider, Freddie Spencer, were to benefit from their own version of the narrow-angle V-twin concept.

Returning to Maico itself, the RS125 continued to be built and was campaigned by riders receiving works backing, such as Jansson. In addition, a large number of privateers used the rapid rotary-valve single to good effect.

This continued well into the 1970s, by which time the quickest bikes were watercooled. This conversion was usually achieved by machining the fins from the head and barrel, then fitting a cast-iron sleeve, various pipes and a radiator.

The factory was also involved in the 250 cc class – not with the SMZ special, but a new 245 cc (76 × 54 mm), rotary-valve, six-speed single. This made its début in 1974.

Originally conceived as a roadster, the 250 was soon used for both production and open-class racing events. In standard trim, it produced 27 bhp at 7800 rpm – around 93 mph. This, together with its

South London lightweight specialist Fred Launchbury (6) rode Maicos for several years in the 125 cc TT during the early 1970s with considerable success

superb handling, was enough to make it competitive in the sports machine class.

The same year also witnessed a full racing version developed by Rolf Minhoff – with the official backing of Maico through its chief designer, Dipl. Ing. Schier.

Mounted in a much lower duplex chassis, the Minhoff-tuned engine pumped out a claimed 43 bhp which, on the road, meant an optimum speed of around 136 mph. However, although outstanding for a single-cylinder design, it was not in the same league as the then class-leading Yamaha TD3 twin.

Even so, the machine gained a considerable amount of attention in the German motorcycling press, which provided Maico with much valuable publicity.

However, from then on, interest in road racing waned, the factory becoming ever more reliant upon its sales of military and off-road competition bikes. Even so, today it is still possible to see the occasional RS125 single giving loyal service in German club events – a lasting tribute to an essentially soundly-engineered, but exceedingly simple design.

10
Münch –
the 'elephant man'

Few men in motorcycling can match the chequered career of Friedl Münch. Ever since he was bitten by the two-wheeled bug as a six-year-old, when his father made him a small motorcycle at his car and motorcycle repair business near Frankfurt, way back in 1933, this enthusiasm has simply kept on growing.

Münch's interest in engineering also blossomed, and after war service as a mechanic with the *Luftwaffe*, he raced a pre-war Horex single for $2\frac{1}{2}$ seasons before damaging his liver in an accident. Then he turned his attention to tuning and produced a competitive racer by converting a pushrod Horex

Regina, with a rev limit of 5500 rpm, into a double-knocker that revved to 7000 rpm. After this came a spell in the Horex race shop during the 1950s, building 250 and 350 singles and the dohc Grand Prix twins. He stayed on until the famous factory foundered during the late 1950s.

His Horex experience was not wasted, however, and besides tuning a number of privately-owned examples, he also sponsored the up-and-coming Klaus Enders on a Norton solo and a sidecar outfit

Ferdinand Kaczor (left) and Friedl Münch (right) with one of the Münch URS fours, February 1970

powered by a Horex Imperator twin with dual-choke Weber carburettor. However, the Horex was becoming obsolete, so eventually Enders took the chance of racing a BMW Rennsport outfit – his first step to becoming a multi sidecar world champion.

During the early 1960s, Münch turned his attention to the design and manufacture of his own racing drum brakes. These potent stoppers soon built up an enviable reputation and, with it, lucrative sales to the racing fraternity – both in Germany and abroad. Used on both solos and sidecars, these superbly-crafted (and powerful!) brakes effectively set Münch on the road to becoming a motorcycle manufacturer in his own right.

The next phase was a four-cylinder, 498 cc racing engine which was completed in early 1964. This dohc, across-the-frame, vertical unit was an extremely neat piece of work, and it proved that Münch could build more than just cycle components.

During the late summer of 1965, Friedl Münch was based in Friedburg, where he was approached by Frenchman Jean Murit. A former sidecar racer and record breaker with BMW machinery, Murit wanted a bike which was faster, stronger and more powerful than any standard production roadster then available from the established manufacturers.

Münch considered the options very carefully before selecting the aircooled NSU Prinz 1000 car engine which had recently come on to the market – thus, the Mammoth was born. Arguably the world's first modern 'superbike' of the type so popular in the 1970s, subsequently, around 500 would be built over the next two decades, the engine size eventually reaching an amazing 1800 cc!

Almost as controversial were the various business partners which the Mammoth attracted over the same period. This was to prompt Münch to say, recently: 'All I ever wanted to do was build motorcycles, but all the people I got involved in business with ever wanted was to take advantage of that and try to get rich quick. I've been cheated, deceived, robbed and lied to – but still today (1988) I'm a happy man because I can still hold my head up and know I never did any wrong to anyone. And most important of all, I'm still making bikes!'

His first business partner was the veteran American motorcycle book publisher, Floyd Clymer. This meant that Münch was able to move from his cramped, stable-like premises to a brand-new factory facility at Ossenheim, which opened in September 1967.

Clymer, a former Indian works rider, had a dream

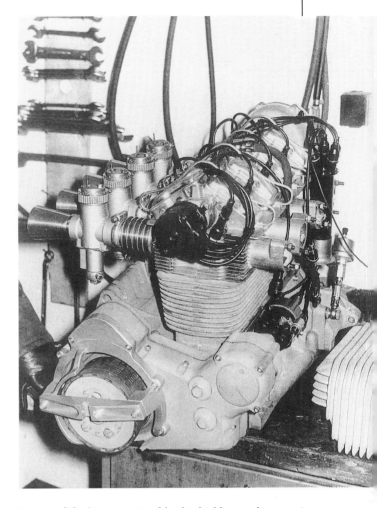

Engine of the 'Daytona Bomb'. This highly-tuned version of the NSU Prinz car engine was built for the express purpose of gaining the legendary one-hour record. Instead, all it did was shred tyres after three circuits of the Daytona speed bowl

of not only assisting Münch to build his Mammoth superbikes, but also relaunching the Indian marque. He had purchased the manufacturing rights to the American machine when the original factory went out of business in 1953.

Normally a shrewd businessman, for once, Clymer acted on sentiment rather than sound commercial judgement. The result was that the reborn Münch-Indian V-twin was a dismal failure.

However, Münch and Clymer continued their partnership, and at the Cologne Motorcycle Show, in September 1968, they unveiled some of their combined handiwork. This included an engine which they announced would be bidding for international racing success.

The new powerplant was a 500 cc, dohc, parallel twin designed and built by Friedl Münch. The pair hoped that it would be battling in the European Grand Prix circus during the following season. Also on display was an sohc version, which was intended to bring success in AMA (American Motorcycle Association) events.

The GP parallel twin, which was not based on Münch's 1964 racing four, had a bore and stroke of 71.5×62 mm. Its double-knocker valve gear was driven by a chain that ran up the centre of the engine; there were four valves and a central spark plug for each cylinder. The crankcase was cast in magnesium, while the heads and barrels were of a new, high-strength, ultra-lightweight aluminium alloy.

Designed in unit with the engine was a five-speed, close-ratio gearbox. Underneath the crankcase was a deeply-finned wet sump which contained six pints of lubricant, but the gearbox and engine oil were separate – unlike the single-overhead-cam production engine. Primary drive was by straight-cut gears, with a dry, six-plate clutch.

Münch experimented with several makes of carburettor, including Amal, Dell'Orto and Weber, with choke sizes ranging from 35 to 40 mm. The show engine, however, was fitted with Amal GPs. Test results had revealed a power output of over 60 bhp at 10,000 rpm as the ultimate target. If the engine proved a success, it was planned to offer it for sale to selected top international-class competitors.

It was stated that the company was planning a thorough test programme throughout the winter months, and the complete machine was scheduled to be ready for race testing later in 1969. A twin-loop cradle frame had already been designed to house the GP engine, although Münch was also seeking assistance from established frame makers. These included the British Rickman brothers, well known for their Metisse chassis. Brand-new telescopic front forks, designed by Münch, had 148 cc of damping oil and boasted a travel of 5.9 in. The now familiar Münch front brake was to be used together with an Italian Fontana at the rear.

Like a modular series of roadsters, powered by the sohc engine ranging from 450 to 750 cc, the double-knocker twin was destined never to see the race tracks. This state of affairs was not helped by Floyd

Münch URS team in April 1970. Left to right: Helmut Fath, Karl Hoppe and Ferdinand Kaczor

Clymer's health, which deteriorated sharply, causing him to retire from the project at the end of May 1969.

It was a well-founded rumour, at the time, that he had sold his entire interest in the Münch factory to an unidentified source, represented by the Chase Manhattan Bank of Frankfurt. Later, it transpired that this mystery backer was an American millionaire's son, George Bell, himself a Münch Mammoth owner. He bought the interest from Clymer's wife as the veteran publisher's health was leaving him. Clymer died in the spring of 1970.

Although, initially, Bell stated that he had intended increasing the production tempo and putting the company on a sound financial footing, it transpired that he saw the Münch enterprise very much as a means of acting the playboy in the world's road-racing circus. Soon, he had Münch working on racing projects rather than production roadsters. As proof of this came a shock announcement, on the front pages of the world's press that September, typified by *The Motor Cycle*, which proclaimed: 'Fath–Münch Tie-up!'

The story behind the headline was the joining of forces by two of Germany's greatest ever special builders – Helmut Fath (1960 and 1968 World Sidecar Champion and creator of the four-cylinder URS) and Friedl Münch (maker of the exclusive Mammoth superbike and his own four- and twin-cylinder racing engines). The man behind this marriage of engineering brains was the American George Bell, who wanted the two to continue producing racing and record-breaking machinery. Bell saw this as a quick route to success, with Münch building the record breaker, and Fath the Grand Prix racer. It should also be mentioned that Bell had already written off the Münch/Clymer dohc, parallel-twin project.

At the beginning of their collaboration with Bell and Münch, Fath and his partner, Dr Peter Kuhn, would continue to operate from their existing premises. However, a brand-new factory, scheduled for completion in the following spring, was being constructed at Altenstadt, near the existing Münch works at Ossenheim. When this was completed, all Münch and Fath interests would be centralized there, and both men would co-operate on racing and roadster projects.

The bike completed during the winter of 1969–70 was a larger-capacity version of the NSU-powered Mammoth for an attack on the world one-hour speed record. This stood at 145 mph and had been gained by Mike Hailwood and MV Agusta.

Karl Hoppe (Münch URS) leads MV star Giacomo Agostini (1) and other riders, Dutch TT, 27 June 1970

Built in the short space of six weeks, the new bike was intended to provide valuable press coverage for the Münch roadsters. Moreover, as Bell was an American from Florida, where better to take this machine and to boost his ego than Daytona? So the 'Daytona Bomb' was born.

The engine from a 1177 cc 1200TTS Mammoth roadster was bored out to 1370 cc – it produced a massive 125 bhp at 8600 rpm. Specially-cast alloy cylinders replaced the original's cast-iron components, but the drive to the camshaft was the same as on the standard engine – by duplex chain up the nearside of the power unit. The 13:1 pistons necessitated the use of rollers to start the brute. Carburation was taken care of by a cluster of four 35 mm Dell'Orto SS1 instruments, each pair being fed from a remotely-fitted float chamber.

Lubrication was taken care of by a semi-dry-sump system, as the crankshaft was not submerged in oil.

To cope with the extra stress, a larger-capacity system was employed, while the lubricant was stored in a separate magnesium sump bolted to the base of the engine. The flywheel was removed, leaving the five-bearing crank to be dynamically balanced after the primary drive pinion had been fitted. This was driven by specially-manufactured helical gears on the nearside of the engine, driving the standard Münch four-speed gearbox via a 12-plate, dry clutch. The last had been considerably enlarged from the standard unit to cope with the increase in output over the roadster.

An additional 10 mm spark plug was provided for each cylinder. The original 14 mm plugs were sparked by a Volkswagen car distributor, which sat at the front of the engine and was driven by a simplex chain with a tensioner pulley on the offside end of the crankshaft. The second set of plugs had their own distributor, mounted on the offside end of the camshaft with 38 degrees advance.

To cope with this vast amount of power, the frame was fitted with the Rickman heavyweight front fork assembly normally employed on Metisse motocross

machines. At the time, this was the only assembly capable of withstanding the demands which would be made upon it, both in terms of weight and speed.

To provide adequate stopping power, Münch's own 250 mm Electron drum brakes were specified, with a four-leading-shoe arrangement at the front.

Following the end of the annual Cycle Week at Daytona, in March 1970, the team, comprising Friedl Münch, Helmut Fath and rider Ferdinand Kaczor, waited for a period of fine weather before proceeding with their initial runs in the last week of the month. When these began, the machine displayed its speed potential by rocketing around the Daytona speed bowl at no less than 178 mph.

But there were snags . . . major snags.

The 'Daytona Bomb' could not keep this up for more than three laps (around nine miles) before the rear tyre tread cried enough and great chunks began to fly off. Even changing tyres for other types did not ease the problem. The result was that there was nothing left to do, but return to Germany in an attempt to persuade the tyre manufacturers to back the project with tyres capable of standing up to the power output and weight of the 1400 cc giant.

As for the bike itself, this stayed in Florida,

Below
First version of the Münch URS outfit, circa 1970

awaiting the outcome of the action. However, through a series of events, it was destined never to make another attempt at the hour record. Instead, it languished in a Miami warehouse for the next 11 years, having been awarded, under a court order, to one of the project's American backers in lieu of payments owed.

Back in Germany, Münch, Kaczor and Fath returned to their respective tasks. For Fath, this meant readying the Münch-URS four-cylinder GP bikes. Their début, under the new colours, came at the non-championship Austrian GP, held over the Salzburg autobahn circuit in late April. Kaczor and the 47-year-old veteran Karl Hoppe made it a 1–2 for the new team, the fastest lap of the meeting going to Kaczor at 87.68 mph.

Two weeks later came the first round in the 500 cc World Championship series. On home ground at Hockenheim, Hoppe finished a respectable fourth. However, more notably at the same event, tensions that had existed, almost from the initial founding by Bell of the Münch-Fath partnership, came to a head. During practice, Münch had insisted that Fath (who was still an active competitor) should race the latest

Horst Owesle, World Sidecar Champion in 1971 and the engineering brain behind the Münch URS racing effort

low-line Münch-URS sidecar outfit. However, Fath objected to this, wanting instead to use his own non-Münch machine. When Münch disagreed with him, Fath announced that he was quitting the team altogether.

To complicate matters further, the team's number-one rider, Kaczor, voiced his intention of going with Fath to race a 350 Yamaha and 500 BMW!

The Münch-Fath dispute had another twist, because when Fath originally agreed to join the team, Bell had, in effect, bought out the whole Fath racing équipe. This meant that even though Fath had not moved all his machinery to the Münch factory in Ossenheim, he was no longer the owner of the remaining hardware.

The result was yet more ill feeling. 'I was cleared out,' stated an upset Helmut Fath afterwards, when he was left with an empty workshop. 'They came with a pantechnicon and cleared out every engine I had.'

Even though Fath and Kaczor had quit, Horst Owesle and Dr Peter Kuhn, who had both worked with Fath before the Münch link-up, stayed with the Münch organization. Although the new partnership did not have any real hope in the 500 cc solo class once Fath had departed, Kuhn did develop a 750 racing four and, with the help of Owesle, went on to garner some great victories on three wheels.

Horst Owesle had been German National Junior Sidecar Champion in 1969 on a BMW. However, no one could have predicted that riding the latest development of the Münch (Fath) URS four-cylinder engine, and partnered by Englishman Peter Rutherford, he would become the 1971 Sidecar World Champion!

Owesle and Rutherford won three of the eight rounds – Holland, Finland and Ulster – finishing in front of a string of BMW Rennsport twins. After this exploit, both Owesle and Rutherford retired from racing, while Englishman Chris Vincent used the four-cylinder outfit during 1972 (finishing fourth in the title hunt).

Credit should also be given to Owesle for his technical expertise. Once Helmut Fath had left, it was he who put on not only leathers, but also overalls to become the team's techical wizard.

The 1971 championship-winning engine was bench-tested at 86 bhp, using four Japanese Keihin carburettors, a higher-lift camshaft and dry-sump lubrication.

The 500 and 750 Münch solos never received the attention of the sidecar machinery, with the result that they languished unused and unloved, except for

Champions Horst Owesle and English passenger Peter Rutherford with the Münch URS outfit, Silverstone, August 1971

the occasional outing. The most notable of these were in Britain, where they were raced occasionally during 1971 by Tony Jefferies.

Racing was to prove the centre of the Bell-funded Münch company's problems. Despite warnings from Friedl Münch himself, Bell sank over half-a-million deutschmarks into the 1971 racing campaign alone, and although Owesle succeeded in taking the World Championship, the factory itself was in dire financial straits. With creditors arriving from all directions, George Bell quickly departed the scene and returned to America, leaving Münch to solve his own problems again.

This he did with the aid of a series of financial backers over the next few years, the story of which is outside the scope of this particular book. However, any dreams he may have harboured of future racing glory went with the departure of the high-flying George Bell. From then on, Friedl Münch was to stick firmly with street-going motorcycles, leaving the glamour of the race circuit to others.

11
MZ – two-stroke technology

Before World War 2, the Saxony town of Zschopau was the home of the most advanced two-stroke motorcycles in the world. DKW (see Chapter 4) had earned the respect of other, predominantly four-stroke, manufacturers with its ultra-quick racing machinery in the years leading up to the outbreak of hostilities in September 1939.

When the conflict was over, the DKW factory was nothing but rubble, and Zschopau found itself in Germany's eastern zone, under the occupation of the Red Army. DKW, therefore, set up shop anew in Ingolstadt, in the western sector, resuming its pre-war activities as best it could.

Meanwhile, from the ashes of the old plant in Zschopau, arose a new addition to the ranks of the world's motorcycle manufacturers, MZ, or to give it full recognition, VEB Motorraderwerke Zschopau.

Although to confuse the issue even more, until the mid 1950s, its products were marketed under the IFA (Industrieverband-Farhzuegebau) label.

The first racing MZ (entered as an IFA) appeared in 1950, four years after the first post-war roadster left the Zschopau production lines. Like its street-going brother, the track bike was a rather unexciting 125 cc single with piston-port induction and a three-speed gearbox. Hardly a motorcycle to provide any hint of the much greater things to come.

The first IFA (MZ) racer appeared in 1950. Developed from its roadgoing brother, it featured piston-port induction, a three-speed gearbox and a massive magneto situated on the offside of the crankcase

Then, in 1951, a private German tuner, Daniel Zimmermann, modified his home-brewed IFA racer by means of a crankshaft-driven rotary disc valve. Thus was ushered in a new era of two-stroke design.

Zimmermann fitted the carburettor directly to the side of the crankcase, where it supplied mixture by means of a disc valve mounted in the crankcase wall. In addition, the cylinder barrel was modified so that the exhaust faced rearwards. Zimmermann also changed the engine's original bore and stroke measurements from 52 × 58 mm to the now widely-used, square 54 × 54 mm dimensions.

The East German riders, Krumpolz and Petruschke, rode Zimmermann-modified bikes to annex fourth and fifth places in the 1951 German Grand Prix. Although not counting towards that year's world championship results, none the less, the event attracted a massive crowd of some 400,000 spectators to the Solitude circuit, near Stuttgart.

The 125 cc event garnered full works entries from DKW, NSU and the Austrian Puch concern, so fourth and fifth positions were an excellent performance. In fact, Krumpolz spent the majority of the race duelling for third place with the vastly-experienced Ewald Kluge, who had won the 1938 Lightweight TT in the Isle of Man on one of the supercharged DKWs.

In fact, Zimmermann's modifications were so successful that MZ quickly took out patents, and subsequent development of the concept was taken over by the engineer Walter Kaaden, who joined the Zschopau factory at the end of 1952. Prior to this,

In 1951 a private tuner, Daniel Zimmermann, modified his home-brewed IFA racer by means of a crankshaft-driven rotary disc valve. The East German riders Krumpolz and Petruschke (167) rode Zimmermann-modified bikes to fourth and fifth places in the 1951 125 cc German GP

Kaaden had built and ridden his own bikes, in the process, gaining experience which was to prove invaluable.

Kaaden set to work for his new employers, and proof of his initial success can be judged from the fact that, at the beginning of the 1953 season, the 125 engine was giving only 9 bhp at 7800 rpm, but at the end of the season, it was pumping out 12 bhp at over 8000 rpm – a healthy 25 per cent increase.

Much of this extra power came from extensive changes to the transfer and exhaust ports, the compression ratio and the exhaust system. In fact, it was this last area that was to be perhaps Kaaden's most significant achievement. It was he who recognized the importance of a highly-resonant exhaust system, combined with the extended port timing made possible by disc-valve induction, coupled with multiple transfer ports and a squish-type combustion chamber.

The MZ's only appearance in the West that year was at the German Grand Prix, held at Schotten. This was boycotted by several factories on the grounds of safety. However, in the 125 cc category, this hardly applied, as MV, NSU and FB Mondial all had riders in action. The sole MZ was that of Krumpolz in ninth

Above

Dieter Krumpolz taking his 125 MZ to ninth position in the 1953 German Grand Prix, held at Schotten. Walter Kaaden had joined the Zschopau factory a few months before, at the end of 1952

position, a lap down on the race winner, Italian Carlo Ubbiali's MV Agusta.

By 1955, Kaaden had developed the disc-valve single to a point where it was almost competitive with the very best of the twin-cam four-strokes. However, his efforts were largely blunted by the international community which, at that time, during the height of the 'cold war', treated East Germany as a leper. Thus, MZ was not only denied the currency to enable it to improve its machines by way of Western components, but also its staff were denied the necessary visas for foreign travel.

Thus, MZ continued to participate only in the two Germanys; the only Grand Prix appearance was at the one held in West Germany each year.

The 1955 event was staged over the famous Nürburgring, the pride of German racing. With its 14.165-mile lap, which rose and fell over nearly 1000 ft, the setting was magnificent with its beautifully-wooded slopes next to the Eifel mountains. It was also the ultimate test of a rider's skill in Continental Europe, with a confusing sequence of

Left

The 1955 125 MZ engine. It featured square (54 × 54 mm) bore and stroke measurements, dual rear-facing exhausts and totally redesigned mechanics

blind bends and undulations that could test even the most experienced pilot's skill.

The 125 cc race was staged over five laps, a total of 70.83 miles. There were 11 finishers, all of whom were mounted on MV Agustas, except Petruschke and Krumpolz, who bought their MZs into fifth and sixth places.

Equipped with full streamlining, the East German 'strokers' were capable of around 95 mph and produced 15 bhp. They had just made the switch from three to four speeds, but were still at a distinct disadvantage on such a demanding circuit compared with the factory MVs, which had a fifth ratio.

In 1956, a youngster named Ernst Degner joined

Right
May 1958, a 125 MZ in the paddock at Hockenheim for the Rheinpokal Rennen races. This machine was ridden by Ernst Degner, who had joined MZ in 1956

Below
By 1956 the works MZs employed full streamlining and six-speed gearboxes. Maximum speed was almost 100 mph

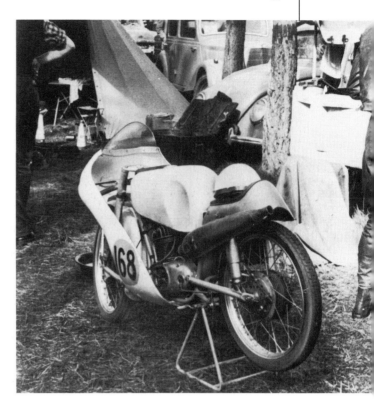

East German mechanics working on a quartet of MZs during the 1958 Ulster GP. They are assisted by their star rider, Degner (centre), who is standing between a pair of the new 250 twins

the team. He was to emerge as the Eastern sector's top rider over the next decade, but he also became involved in a highly controversial affair which rocked the racing world at the end of 1961 – more of this later, however.

For 1956, the German GP returned to the Solitude circuit. The nine-lap, 63.8-mile 125 cc race saw a galaxy of lightweight road-racing talent assembled on the grid. MVs, FB Mondial, Ducati, KTM and the new Gilera twin massed the four-stroke ranks, while the two-stroke flag was flown by DKW, Montesa, Puch and MZ. Against such a formidable line-up, Degner's tenth and the 13th and 14th placings of his team-mates, Fügner and Krumpolz, made a respectable showing. The latest MZs now sported six-speed gearboxes and improved power output over the 1955 bikes.

By 1957, the more informed observers had begun to realize that the small-capacity Zschopau two-strokes were making substantial progress. The season opened with the German GP in May, held over the ultra-fast 4½-mile Hockenheim-Ring.

MZ had three entries: Ernst Degner, Horst Fügner and Werner Musiol. In a race won by Carlo Ubbiali (MV) at an average speed of 99.29 mph, Fügner finished an excellent fourth, Degner sixth and Musiol eighth. This result spurred the MZ design team, led by Kaaden, to even greater effect.

The result was that, at the end of 1957, MZ emerged from Germany's borders for the first time to compete in the Italian GP at Monza. The results of this expedition were nothing to get excited about, as only Degner finished, in seventh position and a lap behind the winner, Ubbiali (MV). However, it was a moral victory, for not only had MZ ventured out of the Fatherland, but Degner's was the first two-stroke across the line. At this stage, the MZ 125 was delivering 16 bhp at 8300 rpm.

Back in the winter of 1953–4, first drawings had been carried out for a completely new MZ, a 250 twin. The broad strategy was to experiment on the 125, then transfer the technology to the twin. (The 250 was actually two 125s with crankshafts spliced to a common primary drive). However, in practice, it was not quite as simple as this, with the result that it was not until 1958 that the larger bike was ready for Grand Prix action.

The setting was the Nürburgring, for only the second Grand Prix to be staged at this venue in the post-war period. First came the 125 cc race. After all three Ducati Desmo riders had been forced out by either accidents or machine trouble in a single lap half-way through the race, it was left to the MZs of Degner, Fügner, Walter Brehme and Musiol to take up the four remaining leaderboard positions behind the two MVs of Ubbiali and Provini. If this was not enough, Fügner gave the twin-cylinder MZ a fabulous début by bringing it home second in the 250 cc race, behind race winner Provini. Fügner's average speed for the six-lap, 85.04-mile race was 73.07 mph (against Provini's speed of 73.94 mph).

At the time of their appearance at the Nürburgring in the spring of 1958, Kaaden's engines were up to the impressive power output of 160 bhp/litre, the 125 producing 20 bhp and the 250, 36 bhp. This also coincided with the factory deciding to take in as many of that year's championship events as possible. With stiff opposition from both MV Agusta and Ducati, the best overall performance came from the 125 single. However, the first ever MZ GP victory came from the 250 twin, ridden by Horst Fügner. It

Works MZ Re125 engine, circa 1957 – compare this with the earlier photographs

Details of the carburettor fitted to the 1958 version of the 125 MZ

took the Swedish round – admittedly, only after Provini was forced to retire.

For 1959, MZ obtained the services of a foreign rider for the first time, in the shape of the widely-travelled Swiss star, Luigi Taveri. It was Taveri who came up with the idea of fitting the front forks from a Manx Norton.

The reason for the adoption of the Norton fork, on the 250 at first, was because with the power output growing, the handling was becoming increasingly poor. This trouble was eventually traced to the front suspension system, and the Norton fork was a great help. Braking on the 250 was another headache. This was due to the combination of speed (by now approaching 130 mph) and the lack of engine braking effect from the two-stroke, twin-cylinder engine. Kaaden's answer to this problem was to design a set of truly excellent drum brakes, the single-sided, single-leading-shoe front one being fitted with a type of centrifugal fan to circulate cooling air through the drum. The rear unit was a single-sided, twin-leading-shoe type.

But how was MZ to acquire stocks of the Norton Roadholder racing fork? The answer came from a chance meeting between the legendary English tuner, Francis Beart, and Kaaden at the 1959 TT. It transpired that Beart had a number of new Norton

Above

MZ signed up the Swiss star Luigi Taveri for the 1959 season. He is shown here in the Ultra-Lightweight (125) TT, in which he finished in runner-up spot

Left

The front forks and brake from a 250 MZ at the 1959 TT. Soon Norton telescopic forks were to become standard ware on the East German bikes. The idea came from Luigi Taveri

Right

Degner before the start of the 1959 250 cc Ulster GP. Note Norton Roadholder forks

Overleaf

The 1959 250 cc Ulster GP was won by the flying Rhodesian Gary Hocking on another MZ, this time sporting the old-style leading-link forks

Above
The 1959 version of the 250 twin-cylinder engine gave almost 40 bhp

Below
The New Zealand rider John Hempleman rode for MZ in the 1960 Isle of Man TT races. He is shown here, on his smaller mount, at Quarter Bridge in the Ultra-Lightweight event

forks at his Guildford tuning establishment. These had been taken from complete machines whose engines he had fitted in Formula 3 cars (Norton would only sell complete bikes!). Beart arranged a trade – forks for brakes – so MZ's lack of Western currency was solved.

Another breakthrough during the same year was Kaaden's adoption of a third transfer port (bridged like its two companions to prevent the single Dykes-type piston ring fouling). Perhaps equally import-ant, however, the side effect of this improved cylinder filling and extra power was the much superior lubrication of what was rapidly becoming a source of unreliability, the caged Ina needle-roller small-end bearing.

Another change was the substitution of the alloy dolphin fairing for a much cheaper and easier-to-construct fibreglass version.

Through 1959, the MZs became ever quicker and more effective as viable top-class Grand Prix machines. The season had started well when Taveri had finished second in the 125 cc TT, with Fügner supplying excellent support in fourth place. When one considers that Taveri was sandwiched between Tarquinio Provini and Mike Hailwood, it can be seen that this was truly a great result.

In the 250 cc race, things were different, as

although well up in the early stages, the MZ trio of Degner, Fügner and Taveri, were all ultimately forced out with mechanical trouble.

Next stop on the championship trail came at Hockenheim, where Degner came home sixth in the 125 race, and Fügner fourth in the 250. At the Dutch TT, MZ had Derek Minter on a 125 (the Kentish rider rode a Morini in the 250 race). Minter was fifth behind team-mate Fügner. In the higher class, Fügner and Degner occupied fifth and sixth positions respectively.

Just before the Swedish GP at Kristianstad, Kaaden acquired the services of the talented Rhodesian Gary Hocking, who had made something of a name for himself with some excellent performances on a pair of single-cylinder Nortons that year. Hocking repaid Kaaden's faith by scoring a victory on his début by winning the rain-lashed 250 cc race by nearly a minute. This was no empty victory, either, as behind the MZ were some of the world's finest riders, men such as Ubbiali, Duke, Hailwood and Dale.

The next GP was in Ulster, where Hocking rode both the 125 single and 250 twin. In the smaller-capacity class, he (and Degner) had to concede to

Start of the 250 cc race at the Halle-Saale circuit, 23 April 1961. The race was won by MZ works rider Werner Musiol (104). Riders 102 and 105 are also MZ-mounted

Mike Hailwood, while the British rider scored his first ever GP victory (aboard his single-cylinder desmo Ducati). In the 250 cc race, however, Hocking turned the tables, beating Hailwood, who was now Mondial-mounted. Again, Degner was third.

After these outstanding results, Count Agusta stepped in and promptly signed up Hocking to contest the final classic, the Italian at Monza. To counter this, MZ obtained the services of Minter (again) and Tommy Robb. Meanwhile, Taveri returned to ride one of the 250 twins. (He had quit MZ to ride for Ducati after the German GP earlier in the year.)

In the 125 race, Degner and Ubbiali fought it out tooth and nail, victory finally going to the German pairing. The same close finish transpired in the 250 cc event, but this time, the Italian won by a matter of inches. After such an excellent end to the 1959 season, much was expected of the MZ team in the following year.

Unfortunately, events did not go according to plan. For a start, after trying to sign various Western riders — Mike Hailwood and Terry Shepherd included — Walter Kaaden eventually settled upon his number-one, home-grown star, Ernst Degner, and the Englishman, Dave Chadwick. This final choice was surprising, as, when the news broke in February 1960, Chadwick was still recovering from a serious arm injury sustained in the previous year's TT.

The German race director said that the main aim of the MZ factory was to win the 125 and 250 cc classes and that Degner and Chadwick would contest all the classic races. He also revealed that MZ intended to

Left
Werner Musiol was born in June 1930, becoming an MZ employee in 1956. Joining the race squad a couple of years later, he rode the 125s and 250s with equal ability

Below
Another of the locally-grown MZ riders was Hans Fischer, seen here on a 125 single in 1961

enter the 350 cc title chase, with an overbored 250. However, these plans received a terrible setback when Dave Chadwick was killed whilst racing a Norton at Mettet, in Belgium, in mid May.

In March, news had come of a new company in Italy, headed by Leopoldo Tartarini, which intended marketing MZ-powered roadsters. To launch the new venture, Tartarini arranged with the East German factory to send some works racers to Italy. In addition, the former Ducati star, Alberto Gandossi, joined MZ. He was to head the Ital-MZ team in Italian events. It also meant that Gandossi would ride in the World Championship series.

The first classic which catered for 125 and 250 cc machines was the Isle of Man TT in early June. Following Chadwick's death, MZ signed up several other 'foreign' riders: the New Zealander John Hempleman and the English trio of Bob Anderson, Dickie Dale and Eddie Crooks.

During the winter months, the development team had been hard at work, the 250 twin-cylinder model receiving most attention. Although basically the same as the 1959 version, it sported a stiffer frame of larger-diameter tubing, while the Norton forks, introduced on a couple of bikes half-way through the previous season, were standardized on all of the 250 cc models. Power output had been stepped up from just over 40 bhp at 10,500 rpm to 45 bhp at

The 1961 250 MZ had many modifications. Most notable of these was the deletion of the rearward-facing exhausts. Instead, Walter Kaaden adopted the more orthodox system with the pipes taken centrally from the front of the cylinders

10,000 rpm. Top speed was in the region of 140 mph.

With the fastest four-stroke twins (MV and Ducati) pumping out slightly less bhp and being significantly heavier at the same time, the latest MZ looked a potential championship winner. Unfortunately, its reliability was to prove abysmal that year, with only four finishes in the top six at the GPs – Hempleman (fourth) and Degner (sixth) in Holland, Dale (fourth) in Germany, and finally, a third place by Degner at the last round at Monza.

Compared to the twin, the 125 single was much more successful. By 1960, its 123.6 cc, six-speed engine was producing a very healthy 23 bhp at 10,700 rpm, while maximum speed was up to 115 mph.

Hempleman and Anderson set the ball rolling by coming home fourth and fifth respectively in the Isle of Man. Then Gandossi placed an excellent third at the Dutch TT. However, it was at the ultra-fast Belgian GP where MZ really proved what a potent bike it had. Degner and Hempleman showed the rest

One of the two prototype 50 cc MZs built in 1962. The one illustrated was watercooled, while the other was aircooled. Their only classic race was the East German GP, but after disappointing results, they were scrapped

of the field the way home, the latter also setting the fastest lap at 101.91 mph.

Degner followed this up with a couple of third positions in the two remaining classics in Ulster and Italy, to finish third in the championships. This was MZ's best position to date.

Meanwhile, development of the new 300 cc MZ had shown that enlarging the two aircooled cylinders had resulted in serious overheating, leading to piston problems.

In December 1960 came the first hint that the up-and-coming Lancashire rider, Alan Shepherd, might be signing for MZ. Confirmation came in late February when a contract was signed. Strangely, Shepherd admitted freely to have never ridden a 125 cc machine, saying, 'I suppose I must be rather unique in that I've signed a works contract to race a class of machine that I've never ridden before.'

Speaking about the 350 cc-class MZ, which had been the problem child of the East German team during the previous year, Shepherd said, 'I believe it's still not ready, but when it is, I expect I'll race it, although it's not mentioned in my present contract.'

However, the run of ill-fortune with its foreign pilots continued, Shepherd being hospitalized following a heavy fall at Imola in late April. A week later, the team, now minus Shepherd, made the journey to Montjuich Park, Barcelona, for the Spanish GP. This was the first round of the 1961 championship series.

The 1961 MZs had many modifications. Most notable was the deletion of the rearward-facing exhaust pipe from the rear of each cylinder. Instead, MZ had adopted the more orthodox system, the exhaust pipe coming out centrally from the front of the cylinder and then curving down and under the crankcase.

Walter Kaaden said that the reason for this move was to give him more latitude when it came to determining exhaust-pipe length – critical in two-stroke racing engines and governed, at that time, by FIM regulations, which stated that exhaust pipes must terminate before the rear of the machine. The latest machines were also fitted with magneto ignition in place of the coil set-up used in 1960, and new frames. On the 250, each cylinder had its own magneto with two sets of contact-breaker points.

Most of the success garnered in 1961 was gained by the revamped 125, which had its best ever year. The single now produced 25 bhp at 10,800 rpm which, on optimum gearing, gave a road speed approaching 120 mph. This level of performance meant that in the 125 cc class, MZ was the bike to beat.

Above
The Hungarian Lazlo Szabo was a double winner in the 1963 Austrian GP. He is shown here on his larger mount

Below
Perhaps the biggest motorcycling news story of 1963 was Mike Hailwood's sensational win in the 250 cc class of the East German Grand Prix, 18 August 1963

Degner set off on the classic campaign trail by finishing second in the Spanish GP. Then he won the Grand Prix of West Germany at an average of just under 100 mph, followed by team-mates Shepherd (now recovered from his Imola injuries), Brehme and Fischer.

Honda-mounted Tom Phillis just managed to pip Degner for victory in the French GP. Then came the Isle of Man. Here, even the gifted Kaaden could do little to prevent the poor showing, due to the inherently temperamental nature of his highly-strung 'strokers' and the uniquely searching character of the long and ultra-demanding $37\frac{3}{4}$-mile mountain circuit. The result was that not a single MZ lasted the distance in either the 125 or 250 cc races.

Back on the shorter Continental GP circuits, the MZ stamina returned and Degner put up some excellent performances. These were headed by victories in East Germany (Sachsenring) and Italy (Monza).

The modified 250 cc watercooled twin-cylinder MZ engine which carried Hailwood to his famous victory in the East German Grand Prix on 18 August 1963

With two rounds left – Sweden and the Argentine – Degner led the 125 cc World Championship. In late September came the Swedish event at Kristianstad, situated in the south of the country. The day dawned with not a cloud in the sky. Before the first race got under way, it had become swelteringly hot, without a breath of air. The four-mile rectangular circuit shimmered in a heat haze. It seemed that nothing, except possibly molten tar, could prevent records being broken.

Right from the first flag-fall, for the 125 cc race, Degner was in business. He was leaving all the other competitors behind within a mile. His screeching MZ had never sounded better. Then, suddenly, after some two-and-a-half laps and 200 yards from the next man, his bike screamed to a halt with a seized engine. However, as his challenger for the world title, Honda's Tom Phillis, had managed to finish no higher than sixth place, Degner still led the championship race.

The drama was not over yet, though, as on the morning following the Swedish GP, MZ's racing chief, Walter Kaaden, was asking 'Where's Ernst Degner?' The truth was that Degner had defected – assisted by members of the Japanese Suzuki management – and had travelled from Kristianstad to

Above
*Alan Shepherd rode this 250 MZ twin to victory in the
United States Grand Prix at Daytona, February 1964*

Right
*The 'spare' engine used by Shepherd for his Daytona
win, after experiencing seizures and broken piston
rings during practice*

Denmark, and thence to West Germany. There, he
joined his wife and two children who had been
smuggled out of East Germany.

This incident caused a political storm, which was
to have severe repercussions for MZ, both on and off
the track. Not only was it robbed of the World
Championship, but Degner's defection meant that
MZ's technology was known to Suzuki. Just how
significant this was can be gauged by the fact that,
until Degner joined the Japanese company, its efforts
at producing racing motorcycles were anything but
successful. In fact, I would go as far as to say that the

Above
Instrument details of Shepherd's Stateside winning machine; water gauge and 0–12,000 rpm Smiths tacho

Below
Ulster Grand Prix, August 1964. Shepherd carefully negotiates the Hairpin following a cloudburst

Suzuki effort had been awful, their machinery being hopelessly slow and exceedingly unreliable into the bargain.

Degner's exit also virtually ended MZ's success in the 125 cc class, and it was to turn more and more to the 250 cc twin in the future. Although in 1962, the Zschopau factory did build a couple of 50 cc singles to contest the new world series introduced for the tiddlers that year. Their only appearance in a classic race, however, was at the Sachsenring in August. One machine was watercooled and the other aircooled. In the hands of Walter Brehme and Dieter Krumpolz, they finished in eighth and ninth places, but they were not competitive against the West German Kreidler or the Japanese works machines and were never seen again.

After years of work with aircooled engines, MZ introduced a semi-liquid-cooled version of its 250 twin in early 1962. This had water jackets around the barrels only to disperse excess heat between the cylinders; the heads remained aircooled. Another change was to pressure lubrication of the main bearings, from the gearbox supply.

Development work on a fully watercooled version was already in hand, and by June 1962, such a machine was ridden in practice, but not raced, at Schleiz. It used twin radiators.

For the East German GP, in mid August, MZ not only had the services of Alan Shepherd, but also the 1961 250 cc World Champion, Mike Hailwood. Ranged against these, in the 250 race, was the entire Honda works team, headed by Jim Redman. In front of 200,000 wildly-excited spectators, Shepherd became the early leader. However, after he was forced out with a broken crankshaft, Hailwood proved that his performance was no fluke by being locked in combat with Redman throughout a sensational race.

In the end, however, even though Hailwood shattered the lap record at 100.78 mph, Redman eventually took the chequered flag by just two tenths of a second.

The performance of the two-stroke twin was on a par with, and sometimes better than, the Japanese

By 1965 the latest version of the MZ Re125 was becoming obsolete, with the arrival of the very latest crop of Japanese multis in the Ultra-Lightweight class

four. For example, although the Honda was faster around the bend prior to the finishing straight, the MZ more than made up the distance on the straight itself.

The 1963 season dawned with the news that Shepherd had signed for the Italian MV Agusta team. This left MZ without the services of a top-line Western rider. Walter Kaaden had tried to sign triple British Champion Derek Minter as a replacement, but this idea collapsed when Minter agreed to ride for the Scuderia Gilera team managed by Geoff Duke.

However, these problems did not stop MZ from getting off in fine style at their first appearance of the 1963 season in Western Europe. MZs swept all before them at the non-championship Austrian GP over the 3.12-mile, semi-autobahn circuit near Salzburg on 1 May.

Both the 125 and 250 cc races were won by a newcomer to the team, Hungary's Lazlo Szabo. Riding a 250 twin, Mike Hailwood hoisted the lap record to over 75 mph before retiring.

With problems of obtaining visas for its East German riders and mechanics, MZ was frustrated once again in its attempt to mount a full Grand Prix challenge. Eventually, it was only able to compete in the two Germanys, Finland and Italy.

The first of these events, the West German GP over the ultra-fast 4.8-mile Hockenheim circuit, at the end of May, saw Szabo take an excellent third place in the 125 cc race, while Shepherd, who had fallen out with MV, was back in the MZ camp and scored sixth. In the 250 cc race, the twin-cylinder models were down the field in sixth (Szabo) and seventh (Shepherd).

Left
Although he did not score any GP victories, Woodman gave MZ sterling service for three seasons (1965, 1966 and 1967), a third position in the 1965 125 cc World Championship perhaps being the highlight

Overleaf
The East German Heinz Rosner became MZ's team leader in 1968. He is pictured in the 250 cc race, leading Phil Read into La Source Hairpin, Belgian GP, July 1968

Below
After Alan Shepherd signed for Honda at the end of 1964, MZ recruited his fellow Lancastrian Derek Woodman. He is shown here at Sulby Bridge during the 1965 125 cc TT

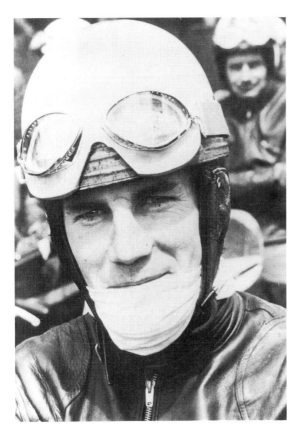

East German GP, 1968. The 125 MZs of Günther Bartusch (170) and Lazlo Szabo (148) lead a quartet of other Zschopau singles at Hohinstien-Ernsthal

On 22 June, three East German MZ works riders were injured during a multiple pile-up at Opatija, Yugoslavia. This left Hans Fischer with a broken wrist and Wolfgang Moses with a fractured skull, whilst Horst Enderlein sustained a broken leg.

Without doubt, however, the biggest MZ news story of 1963 was Mike Hailwood's sensational win in the 250 cc class of the East German GP at Sachsenring in August.

Motor Cycling summed it up thus: 'Two hundred thousand East Germans rose to their feet shouting, cheering and waving flags as Mike Hailwood scored the most popular win of his fabulously successful career at the Sachsenring on Sunday. Piloting a locally built MZ two-stroke twin in the East German Grand Prix, Mike had spreadeagled the opposition to win the 250 cc class at a record speed of 98.30 mph.'

To add to the delight, MZs also filled second (Shepherd) and fourth (Szabo) places on the leaderboard.

The reason behind much of this success was the work carried out by Kaaden and his team during the winter of 1962–3, which had lifted the power output to 48 bhp at 10,800 rpm. A single, light-alloy radiator and finning on the water jackets were used. However, the fins were for strength, not cooling. A new crankshaft had also been introduced following Shepherd's retirement during the 1962 East German GP. Incidentally, this was the first time a 250 MZ had succumbed to bottom-end failure. More usually, the retirement had been caused by piston seizures.

As already related, the early experimental engines had had sheet-metal jackets simply welded around an existing cylinder after the fins had been ground away, while the cylinder head remained aircooled. For 1963, the change was made to watercooling of both the cylinder and head, using entirely new components. Water circulation was provided by the thermo-syphon method with no water pump. When the engine was running, heated water inside the cooling jacket would rise and flow up through a large-diameter hose to the top of the radiator, where it would displace cooler water that would flow downward, through another hose, and into the cylinder jacket.

MZ had also reverted to rearward-facing exhausts. It had been found that with the exhaust ports at the front, any slight gain from having an increased exhaust-pipe length to play with was more than offset by the drop in power output and decreased reliability.

Another reason for positioning the exhaust port at the rear of the cylinder had been to improve piston sealing (with a forward-rotating engine, rod angularity during the power stroke pushes the piston against the rear cylinder wall), as there had been a noticeable power loss with the relocated exhaust port. Most damning of all, however, was that the forward-port engines proved even more prone to piston seizures! This was probably caused by the reduced sealing effectiveness allowing some of the flame to blow down past the piston on the exhaust-

port side. This caused overheating of the piston and, additionally, burned away the lubricant on that side of the cylinder.

Finally, the power output was raised from the 1962 figure of 46 bhp to 48 bhp, while fuel consumption at racing speeds was in the region of 22 mpg.

One other major problem still remained unsolved – the political one. There is no doubt that this, combined with the shoestring budget within which MZ race development had to work, was a great and unseen handicap.

Even with these problems, MZ attempted to step up its World Championship challenge in 1964. Thus, it was decided to provide as much backing as possible to its number-one runner, Alan Shepherd.

In practice, this meant that the Englishman was left very much to his own devices, as it was still not possible for factory mechanics to be with him at the vast majority of meetings.

MZ works rider Heinz Rosner during the 350 cc race of the 1968 Czech Grand Prix; he finished second. Note the cobbled road surface and unprotected brick walls

The 1969 MZ 250 twin pumped out well over 50 bhp from its disc-valve, six-speed motor, giving a maximum speed of around 140 mph

When one realizes that Shepherd was very much a 'one man band' – rider and spannerman – his achievement of finishing third overall in the 1964 250 cc World Championship, against the combined might of Honda, Suzuki and Yamaha, was impressive to say the least.

Shepherd and MZ got off to a flying start at the United States Grand Prix at Daytona. Although his engine seized and broke piston rings during practice, he used a spare motor to take victory at record speeds. He followed this by finishing second in the Isle of Man, third in Belgium, fourth in Ulster and fifth in Italy.

For the TT, a new, lower Featherbed-type frame was built. In addition, a new double front brake appeared. Power was upped to 53 bhp at the lower engine speed of 10,400 rpm.

Then, detail development over the following winter raised the output still further by 1 bhp, while peak revs rose to 10,900 rpm. At the same time, a 350 cc-class machine was at last made available, but with a capacity of only 251 cc (Hailwood débuted the new bike with a superb second in the Japanese GP). However, most work went into making the machines handle better and a weight-reduction exercise.

For a start, the 1965 twins were 100 mm (4 in.) narrower, with new frames and 18 in. wheels at both ends. A slimmer fairing was also constructed.

Other modifications aimed at improving reliability were the use of British Lucas transistorized ignition, which replaced the ancient IKA magneto; a one-piece crankshaft, which was not only stronger, but with less flex meant that ignition timing was more accurate; and, finally, interconnected cylinders with common breathing to improve the carburation.

By now, the 125 cc single was becoming obsolete, following the arrival of the very latest crop of Japanese multis in the Ultra-Lightweight class.

During the 1964 Italian GP, at Monza, Alan Shepherd had signed to ride for Honda in the following year. His MZ swan-song was at Scarborough in mid September, when he achieved a double on works MZs in the 125 and 250 cc races. The following month, fellow Lancastrian Derek Woodman was signed as a replacement.

In January 1965, it was revealed that MZ had a brand-new, three-cylinder, 125 cc racing engine. Work on this new project had begun in April 1964. It featured disc-valve induction and was aircooled. The configuration was that of a vertical twin, with an extra cylinder in the middle. Although several arrangements were tested before the definitive prototype was finally selected, all had three separate carburettors. In theory, being a two-stroke, the MZ was the equal of a six-cylinder four-stroke of the same capacity.

Definitive version of the long-running twin, as it appeared for the 1971 season

Unfortunately, the triple never made it to a Grand Prix – ignition troubles and an ultra-tight power band finally sealed its fate. Instead, MZ carried on with its ageing 125 single and 250 twin, with the odd outing in the 350 cc class on an overbored 250.

Although he did not score any GP victories, Woodman gave sterling service to MZ for three seasons (1965, 1966 and 1967). The highlight was a third position in the 1965 125 cc World Championship.

After Woodman left, it was the East German Heinz Rosner who took up the mantle. Then, in the early 1970s, the Italian Silvio Grassetti rode for a while, in the process, scoring a couple of GP victories.

Italian Silvio Grassetti gave MZ a couple of Grand Prix victories during the early 1970s. He is seen here on the 250 during the Finnish GP, 30 July 1972

However, the chance for real glory had passed MZ by, for the massive Japanese racing effort of the mid-late 1960s had simply been too great for a company with only limited resources, such as MZ – even if it had an engineer of truly rare quality in the shape of Walter Kaaden.

At least both man and factory can take comfort from the indisputable fact that it was they, and not the mighty Japanese, who pioneered the modern, high-performance, two-stroke engine.

12
NSU – racing and records

Road racing

The NSU story began in 1873, when a couple of engineers, Heinrich Stroll and Christian Schmitt, set up a modest business, specializing in the manufacture and repair of knitting machines, at the small town of Riedlingen, on an island in the channel of the River Danube. This enterprise was so successful that by the following year, the company moved once more. In 1880, however, the partners decided to go their separate ways. It was Schmitt who established his new business – still based firmly around the

manufacture of knitting machines – at the town of Neckarsulm, so named because it was here that the two rivers of the Neckar and Sulm met.

Although Christian Schmitt died some four years later, at the early age of 39, his brother-in-law, Gottlob Banzhaf, took over the reins and soon fulfilled one of his predecessor's dreams, that of manufacturing bicycles. The first year these were produced was 1889, and by 1892, the company's main source of revenue was from the new product. That year also saw the first pedal cranks produced – a successful line that was to continue, almost unbroken by two world wars and various financial upheavals, until as late as 1960.

Banzhaf was nothing if not innovative, and he was not a man to stand still very long. Soon, the manufacture of knitting machines was phased out, to be replaced by the exciting prospects of how best to utilize the invention of the internal combustion engine for powered two-wheelers.

By 1900, these experiments had reached a satisfactory stage, and the company (now called NSU – Neckarsulm Strickmachen Union) had produced its first prototype, production commencing in 1901. In this year, an NSU powered by a Swiss-made Zedel engine became Germany's first motorcycle, in the accepted sense of the word, to be marketed on a commercial basis.

NSU soon sought export markets for its motorcycles, including Britain, where a sales organization was established.

The Neckarsulm marque never looked back and soon took an active interest in the sporting side, building its first racing machine in 1905, and competing in the very first Isle of Man TT races in 1907. The bike was ridden by Martin Geiger, NSU's

The fearsome 498 cc version of the pre-war supercharged 348 cc twin. Such machines were used until 1951 when Germany rejoined the FIM

German sidecar and solo champions respectively: Hermann Böhm (left) and Wilhelm Herz. Both used NSU machinery

manager in Britain, to fifth place in the single-cylinder class.

Up to the outbreak of World War 1, the company continued to expand. However, the conflict saw Neckarsulm, like similar engineering plants, heavily engaged in the war effort and turning out munitions between 1914 and 1918. With the war over, NSU rapidly returned to peacetime pursuits.

The Neckarsulm factory pioneered 'production-line' techniques in the German industry during 1929, which also saw the appointment of the famous English designer, Walter Moore – the man who had designed the first overhead-camshaft Norton, which appeared in 1927. That year also saw the start of the great Depression, which nearly killed off the firm, but it survived by the skin of its corporate teeth.

From 1932 onwards, the rebirth began, and in 1938, the company had its best year yet, when nearly 63,000 motorcycles were produced. It was also the year which heralded the technically-advanced, supercharged, 344.82 cc (56 × 70.5 mm),

double-knocker, parallel twin racer. Power output was 68 bhp, giving a maximum speed of almost 125 mph.

When NSU went to war, for the second time, it was put to various tasks, including making aviation components, motorcycles and one of the oddest vehicles ever seen, the Kattenkrad (chaintrack motorcycle). This was a small, tracked, personnel carrier, which inherited its steering (and front wheel) from a conventional motorcycle, whereas the rear section was similar to a tank!

With the end of hostilities in 1945, the various production facilities belonging to the company were almost completely wrecked, as they had represented prime targets for the Allied bombing campaign. In the first couple of years of peace, NSU manufactured almost anything to survive, but even so, it was luckier than rivals such as DKW, who had ended the war in the Russian sector – at least Neckarsulm was in the West.

This enabled NSU to be at the very forefront of the rebirth of the German motorcycle industry, and by 1948, albeit in relatively small numbers, production, was under way on a full commercial basis. During this period, a return was made to racing. Walter Moore, who had left at the outbreak of war,

The Albert Roder-designed R54 500 four-cylinder racer made its début in April 1951; a change of policy saw the project scrapped at the end of that year

had been succeeded as chief designer in 1947, by Dipl. Ing. Albert Roder. His first move had been to enlarge the pre-war supercharged 350 twin to 500 cc (499 cc – 63 × 80 mm). It was with these machines that the likes of Heiner Fleischmann, Wilhelm Herz and Walter Zeller challenged the supremacy of the supercharged BMWs in those early post-war years within the German borders (supercharging was banned in the rest of Europe by that time).

However, in readiness for Germany's re-admittance by the FIM, which would mean that blowers could not be used, chief engineer Roder began to consider other designs. The first of these was the 500 four-cylinder project, which began when Roder took part in an Alpine publicity tour aboard the newly-introduced 98 cc Fox roadster in the summer of 1949. In Switzerland, he made a point of staying in Berne to watch the Swiss GP, held over the Bremgarten circuit. The machines which held his attention were the four-cylinder Gileras of Artesiani

and Pagani, which finished the 500 cc race in second and fourth places respectively.

Upon his return to Germany, Roder set about drawing up two designs – one with, and one without, supercharging. Both shared the same 494.68 cc (54 × 54 mm) engine capacity.

The début of the dohc four, coded R54, did not take place until May 1951. This was when one of the machines was ridden at the annual Eilenriede-Rennen races.

Subsequently, the R54 was used in numerous German events during the 1951 season, being ridden by works riders Herz and Fleischmann, while development continued. The engine was also used in sidecar events by the national champions, Böhm and Fuchs. However, although this development programme was going to plan, it was decided, at senior management level, to scrap the four-cylinder model and, in its place, design new machinery for the smaller classes (125 and 250 cc)

However, the lessons learned with the four were not wasted, and the new bikes derived considerable technical benefit from the R54.

June 1951 saw the appearance of the first of the lightweight racer designs, the 125 R11 Rennfox. Like the 500 R54, it employed square 54 × 54 mm bore and stroke dimensions, which equated to a capacity of 123.67 cc. Power output of the double-overhead-cam single was 12 bhp at 10,500 rpm. It had a forged, three-ring, 9.8:1 compression piston and Amal RH9 26 mm carburettor.

The Rennfox engine was an extremely neat piece of engineering, with a vast cambox, extensive use of aluminium and full unit-construction. A mass of gears on the offside of the unit transmitted power to the head via a bevel shaft. There was also another gear assembly with a conventional pressed-up crankshaft and one-piece connecting rod with a roller-bearing big-end. Integral with the crankcase was a massive oil chamber for the wet-sump lubrication system. External plumbing for the pump was in the form of braided stainless-steel hoses. A large oil filler cap protruded from the engine alongside the forward-mounted magneto drive pinion. The cylinder head and barrel were inclined 12 degrees from vertical.

The engine assembly was housed in a pressed-steel frame, based on the Fox roadster, with leading-link front forks. These were controlled by an external damper, while at the rear was a form of monoshock suspension without rebound damping. Brakes were aluminium-alloy, full-width drums, front and rear, which carried flanges secured by rivets for the alloy wheel rims. The bike's appearance was dominated by the exhaust system. Its long, shallow-taper megaphone ran back on the offside, almost as far as the extreme rear of the machine. A neatly-crafted, 14-litre, alloy tank, proclaiming 'Fox NSU', provided a final touch to the flyweight speedster.

Above right
Front end from the R54. The forks are noteworthy for their curved legs, rubber suspension units and individual cast-aluminium trailing links

Right
June 1951 saw the first appearance of a brand-new 125 racer. The R11 Rennfox was the first of the machines which benefited from technology gained from the abortive four-cylinder design

Overleaf
Roberto Columbo was one of two Italians in the NSU works team of 1952. He is shown in winning form on the Rennfox that year

Above
Nürburgring, August 1952. An interesting view of dual petrol and oil tanks with their respective 'snorkel'-type breathers, as fitted to a 125 works Rennfox

Below
Another view of the same machine, showing the engine, suspension and brakes

However, Roder was not satisfied, so for 1952 the Rennfox received a significant facelift – although underneath, it had much in common with the original.

Major changes which were clearly visible included the dry clutch and a front suspension with new-style leading links and integral hydraulic spring/damper units, plus revised brakes with the operating lever on the nearside. Engine changes encompassed a shallower sump and vertically-mounted oil pump, delivery from which was via a cast-in feed to flexible hoses on top of the offside casting. A four-stud-fixing blanking plate covered the magneto drive pinion. Less evident was the engine tuning, with power upped to 14 bhp at 11,000 rpm.

During the 1952 season, there were other alterations, including a new rear fork controlled by twin, external-spring, hydraulically-damped suspension units. Massive 'snorkel tube' breathers were added at the front of the combined fuel and oil tank.

April that year had seen NSU advertise for riders for its factory racing team – it received 274 applications! It finally selected six: Otto Daiker, Wilhelm Hofmann, Hubert Luttenberger, Walter Reichert, plus two Italians, Romolo Ferri and Roberto Columbo.

The début of the new bike and its riders came at

Prototype 250 Rennmax twin during test programme, summer 1952

Hockenheim on 11 May 1952, when Ferri, Hofmann, Luttenberger and Reichert came home third, fourth, fifth and sixth in the 125 cc event. However, although the Rennfox displayed remarkable reliability for a brand-new design, it clearly could not match the speed of the FB Mondials, which finished in front of them.

It was the 250 cc race which attracted the most attention, though, with works entries from DKW, Moto Guzzi and NSU. The last was one of the best-kept secrets for years, and the R22 Rennmax dohc parallel twin was destined to prove one of the all-time greats of motorcycle racing.

Unlike the 125 Rennfox, the twin was the work of Dipl. Ing. Walter Froede. The 1952 Rennmax shared the square 54 × 54 mm dimensions of both the 125 single and 500 four, giving a capacity of 247.34 cc. At first, the power output was 25 bhp at 9000 rpm, improving to 29 bhp at 9800 rpm by the season's end.

The engine was also of full unit-construction, with primary drive by enclosed chain to a four-speed, close-ratio gearbox. It employed a pressed-up crankshaft assembly supported by a trio of roller bearings. Premature failure of light-alloy big-end cages at high engine speeds was eliminated by the use of an improved alloy and by anodizing the friction surfaces. There was an Alfin cylinder barrel with an aluminium-alloy head. The twin overhead camshafts were driven on the offside of the engine by separate 'Y'-bevel shafts, as they had been on the earlier 350/500 dohc parallel twins. A particular feature of the early 250 was the use of torsion-bar valve springs, but after problems, these were soon relegated to the scrap bin and replaced by the more conventional hairpin type. These remained thereafter on all the later Rennmax variants.

Two single-float-chamber, 24 mm (later 25 mm) Amal RN carburettors were fitted, with 30 degrees of downdraught. As on the smaller design, both exhaust megaphones were of the long, shallow-taper type. Sparks were provided by a battery/coil system. Twin 6-volt, 7-amp/hour batteries, wired in parallel, were housed in a light-alloy pressing beneath the seat. The use of coil ignition on the Rennmax was not due to any desire to economize

Above

Offside of prototype Rennmax. Note the Y-plan camshaft drive, distributor ignition and German Amal carb

Below

This nearside view shows the tacho drive from the exhaust cam, hairpin valve springs and air scoop in the outer engine cover to direct cooling air to the clutch

upon the small amount of power absorbed by a magneto. Instead, it was dictated by repeated magneto problems encountered in the early stages of development with the Rennfox single. A distributor, housing the points and condenser, was mounted in the timing chest and driven by a skew gear from the lower bevel of the inlet camshaft drive coupling.

A full-cradle, twin-downtube, tubular frame was specified. It was equipped with twin-shock, swinging-arm suspension and telescopic front forks (the Rennmax was the only post-war NSU racer to use them).

Other details included an aluminium-alloy fuel tank, full-width SLS brake hubs and 18 in. alloy wheel rims. On some of these early Rennmax models, a large, hand-beaten alloy tail fairing was fitted, but on other examples, the rear end was left naked.

Development of both the Rennfox and Rennmax continued apace throughout the summer of 1952, NSU technicians working to ensure that their brainchildren would be truly competitive for a real crack at World Championship honours the following year. At that time, the NSU racing department was one of the largest and most comprehensive in the world. Housed in a building divorced from the main factory, Dipl. Ing. Froede, together with a staff of ten engineers, office personnel and some 40 mechanics, ensured that the machines they produced were among the very best available at that time.

Another important step towards championship honours came with the discovery of a new star, Werner Haas. Born at Augsberg in 1927, Haas had served his racing apprenticeship aboard an Austrian Puch split single. In his first big race for NSU, he displayed real class and potential by winning a star-studded 125 race, beating such well-known names as Carlo Ubbiali and Cecil Sandford in the process.

Haas was the first to exploit the Rennmax twin when, in the Italian GP at Monza, he stormed round to finish second to the 1952 250 cc World Champion, Enrico Lorenzetti!

In December, it was announced that the Derbyshire rider, Bill Lomas, had signed to race 125 and 250 cc NSUs for the 1953 season. The complete team was to comprise Lomas, Daiker, Luttenberger and Haas.

Evidence of how serious was NSU's quest for honours can be gauged by the fact that Lomas and Haas were sent to the Isle of Man some ten weeks prior to the start of that year's TT. This was to allow Haas to learn the circuit from the experienced Lomas. For these sessions, both teacher and pupil rode standard Max roadsters.

German GP at Schotten, 19 July 1953. NSU works rider Otto Daiker in action during the 125 cc event

Over the winter months, development had continued, and when Lomas débuted the latest Rennmax twin at the Belgian Floreffe meeting, in April, it showed that the time had been put to good use. Leading from start to finish, Lomas finished almost six minutes in front of the second man home, the Guzzi privateer Faucheraux, after Fergus Anderson on the latest four-valve, twin-carb, works Guzzi had retired.

In appearance, the 1953 Rennmax was considerably changed from the original version, which had been campaigned in the previous year. A brand-new, pressed-steel chassis, leading-link front forks, and aluminium wrap-around 'bikini' fairing and fuel tank were just some of the more noticeable differences. In the engine department, the compression ratio had been upped to 9.8:1 which, together with larger 25.4 mm Amal RN9 carburettors and revised cam profiles, had resulted in the power rising to 32 bhp at 10,000 rpm.

A fortnight after Floreffe, at Hockenheim, Lomas again led the 250 race, but this time he was destined to retire. Haas, however, completed an impressive NSU double by taking both the 250 and 125 races.

The latter was on a 1953-type Rennfox single which, like its larger brother, had been completely revised.

The latest 125 single-cylinder engines were smaller externally and of a different appearance to the 1952 type. The vertical coupling (bevel shaft) to the overhead cam was on the nearside of the cylinder instead of the offside, as on the original. Moreover, the old Rennfox's 'square' engine finning had been superseded by a new round-look head and barrel with the revised 58 × 47.3 mm bore and stroke dimensions. Another notable difference was that coil ignition had been selected, as on the twins, and the contact-breaker was driven by a worm gear from the crankshaft coupling. The frame on these machines was a composite of pressed steel and tubular steel. It was completed by hydraulically-damped front and rear suspension. At Hockenheim, a single overhead camshaft was used, but later machines employed dohc, following yet more development. In addition, engine cooling arrangements, brakes, suspension and streamlining all received attention as the season unfolded.

Following Hockenheim came the IoM TT. Here, NSU had entered two riders – Lomas and Haas – for both the Ultra-Lightweight (125) and Lightweight (250) races. Unfortunately, both suffered crashes in practice. Although Haas was unharmed, the English

Above
Scene in the NSU workshop, 1953 TT. A 125 Rennfox is on the ramp, while a 250 Rennmax is on the floor

Right
Triple World Champion and NSU team leader Werner Haas was arguably Germany's finest post-war racer

rider received more serious injuries and, thus, was prevented from racing (it also meant an end to his association with the Neckarsulm marque).

Against formidable opposition, Haas finished second in both races – quite sensational when one considers that these were his first events over what was by far the most demanding of all the world's road racing circuits.

The double-overhead-cam Rennfox engine was first seen during practice for the TT, and was first raced at the next championship round in Holland. There, Irishman Reg Armstrong supplemented the team in the 250 cc category, while Dickie Dale rode a 125.

Over the famous Assen course, Haas showed a clean pair of heels, on both his mounts, to give NSU its first double Grand Prix success. This set the scene for the remainder of the year, with Haas not only

A 1954-type Rennmax twin at Floreffe, Belgium, in May that year

becoming the first German to carry off a world championship, but also only the second rider to achieve a double, in spite of extremely strong competition from other machines and riders. Perhaps most amazing of all, however, was that prior to 1952, he had been completely unknown, even in his native country.

He achieved his championship with victories on the 125 at Assen, Dundrod and Monza, plus runner-up positions in the Isle of Man and at Schotten. On the larger model, he scored wins at Assen and Schotten, with runner-up positions in the Isle of Man, Ulster and Italy.

Armstrong also showed up very well, coming second in the 250 cc Championship with victories in Ulster and Switzerland. Originally, his participation in the Assen race had been a 'one-off', as a stand-in for the injured Lomas. However, his excellent showing, and the fact that Lomas took longer to recover than expected, saw the Irishman promoted to a full team member.

It was very much Haas' year. Not only was he double World Champion, but he became double German champion into the bargain!

To cap a truly magnificent year, Werner Haas was also voted Germany's 'Sportsman of the Year' for 1953. Among the many guests at the NSU works, when Haas was presented with a new Mercedes car by the management, was Tommy Bullus, the Englishman who had ridden NSUs to countless victories during the 1930s.

March 1954 brought the news that the entire works team for the forthcoming classics, except Reg Armstrong, was on the Isle of Man for course instruction by team leader Werner Haas. His pupils were all newcomers: Hans Baltisburger, Hermann Müller and the Austrian Ruppert Hollaus.

The following month, at Floreffe, the latest Rennmax took its public bow. As before, this meeting was intended very much as a shake-down before the more serious work got under way at the classics.

The wisdom of this move was proved when a number of teething problems were revealed. Furthermore, the gusty conditions, during both practice and racing, provided the NSU team with a realistic idea of how its revised streamlining might behave on the mountain sections of the TT course.

NSU engineers were also keen to see how the 'new' Rennmax would perform in combat, as it had been the centre of a major redesign over the winter months. By that time, Dipl. Ing. Froede was beginning to appreciate both the value of efficient streamlining and the benefits of volumetric efficiency, that is the most effective way of filling the cylinders and burning the charge of gas to produce the most power. Therefore, to this end, the engine was extensively redesigned with larger valves and bigger

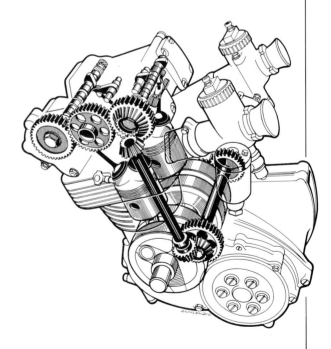

Technical details of the revised Rennmax twin that was raced during the 1954 season. Most notable is its camshaft drive, which employed a single shaft and had been transferred from the offside to the nearside

Above
'Bird-beak' streamlining, as used during the early part of 1954 by the NSU team

Below
The Rennmax was not the only engine to receive major changes – the 125 Rennfox single was also the subject of major revision. Compare this late 1953 motor with earlier illustrations

carburettors. The most noticeable difference between the new twin-cylinder engine and its predecessor was that the latter's separate shafts and bevel overhead-cam drives, which were on the offside of the engine, had been replaced by a single shaft on the other side, at the rear of the cylinder. In turn, this drove the inlet cam and was driven from the intermediate gear of the primary train. Spur gears transmitted the drive from the inlet cam to the exhaust camshaft.

The bore and stroke were altered to 55.9×50.8 mm (249.3 cc) in the interests of reducing piston friction. The crankshaft became a five-piece, pressed-up unit, which was clamped together with Hirth couplings and supported in a quartet of roller-bearings. Power was taken from a central gear pinion and transmitted via a five-speed gearbox. A manual timing override was provided for the rider to operate, up to a massive 40 degrees of advance at the peak of 11,500 rpm. At that figure, the engine produced a class-beating 39 bhp, and the maximum speed of an unfaired machine was in the region of 125 mph. With the 1954 streamlining fitted, an extra 10 mph was on tap.

Battery/coil ignition was retained, while the spine frame was little altered from the 1953 design, as were the forks and rear suspension. However, the rear subframe structure was constructed from pressings instead of tubing. In addition, the front forks had been lengthened to improve suspension geometry. Front brake torque reaction, as before, was transmitted to the structure by a tension strut, but the brake operation was on the nearside of the hub. Both brakes had twin leading shoes.

Formally, the streamlining of the Rennmax consisted of a front mudguard with side valances extending to the hub, a faired rear mudguard and a steering-head fairing that extended rearward, below the rider's arms, and embodied a small, curved windscreen. Taking into account a relaxation of FIM regulations on mudguarding, a front one was no longer fitted, and shielding for the front wheel was provided by the streamlining. The shape of the NSU aluminium cowling was reminiscent of the previous season's Moto Guzzi type, with its 'bird-beak' projection over the front wheel. However, the NSU variation completely embraced the handlebar and extended downwards to the base of the engine to shield the rider's arms and legs.

Cooling air for the engine and exposed clutch entered through an opening in the front of the

Works 125 Rennfox at Hockenheim, May 1954

Above
*A pre-production 250 Sportmax ohc single at
Hockenheim, 1954. The rider was Walter Reichart*

Right
*H. P. 'Happy' Müller, the surprise winner of the 1955
250 cc World Championship title with his semi-
factory Sportmax*

cowling, and improved airflow over the rider's head
and shoulders was provided by an increase in the
height and width of the curved windscreen. Extensive use had been made of the wind-tunnel facilities
at the Stuttgart Technical College to establish the
optimum curvature for the fairing.

Some observers likened the resultant profile to a
dolphin's snout. NSU mechanics accordingly
dubbed it the 'dolphin'. Later, in 1958, when the
FIM banned full fairings, 'dolphin' was the term
used to describe the new type of permissible fairing.

Although the basic dohc 125 Rennfox engine
design had remained unchanged, the power output
had risen to 18 bhp at 11,500 rpm. As before, a six-
speed gearbox was employed because of the need to
keep the engine on the boil. Now, however, as a
result of improved streamlining and increased

Müller and Sportmax in action. Note alloy full 'dustbin' streamlining

power, maximum speed was some 5 mph faster. Twin-leading-shoe brakes were specified for both wheels, but even so, the weight had been pruned back from 83.5 kg (184 lb) to 80 kg (177 lb).

The 1954 Rennfox's frame had been revised and carried similar streamlining to the latest Rennmax. At first, this meant a 'dolphin' design with a large-capacity, hand-beaten alloy fuel tank and tail fairing. However, this was to be replaced, mid season, by an ugly, full dustbin with 'droop snout', followed by the more shapely 'blue whale' streamlining.

The first round of the 1954 world title hunt was held at the French Reims circuit. This was a complete walk-over for NSU, which was the only official works team in the 250 cc race – there was no 125 event.

The real business came at the TT, a couple of weeks later. However, NSU still completely dominated the 250 event, Haas, Hollaus, Armstrong, Müller and Baltisburger taking the first five places! In the 125 event, Hollaus won and Baltisburger was fourth.

The NSU works team presented a formidable air of confidence wherever it went that year. Its sheer professionalism was unmatched in the classic era.

For example, the team would stage the most intimidating pre-race ritual. This involved pre-heating the oil for the engines and warming the engines with heated air, delivered by yards of massive trunking. It impressed many, including a certain Soichiro Honda who, years later, was to base his own works team around the NSU ideal (see *Classic Japanese Racing Motorcycles*, Osprey Publishing). This awe not only applied to the team's organization, but also to the machinery itself which, that year, simply steam-rollered the opposition in the lightweight categories.

In the first four rounds of the 1954 World

Sportmax as sold to paying customers. In its day, it was the quickest non-works machine money could buy in the 250 class

Championship series (the IoM TT, Ulster GP, Dutch TT and German GP 125 cc; and the French GP, IoM TT, Ulster GP and Dutch TT 250 cc), NSU machines simply swept the board in both lightweight classes. By the fifth rounds, neither Haas (250) nor Hollaus (125) could be overtaken in their respective leading positions in the championship tables. This was one of the most impressive showings by any factory in the history of the World Championships.

With the 250 Rennmax often winning in a faster time than the 350 cc race leader, several observers foresaw the next development, which made its public début at the German national championship at the Noris-Ring, Nürnburg on 1 August 1954. This was a 288 cc version of the Rennmax, ridden by Hermann Müller. All that had been done to the engine was to increase the stroke, giving dimensions of 55.9 × 60 mm. This one modification raised the power to 40.4 bhp at 11,200 rpm. Not only did the stroked Rennmax win against such formidable opposition as the works DKW team and Ray Amm's factory Norton, but its average speed of 76.94 mph was only 0.13 mph slower than Amm's winning

speed in the *500 cc* race. Moreover, it set the fastest lap of the meeting at 79.36 mph.

At the time, NSU's team boss, Germer, stated that it was 'factory policy only to use these larger Rennmax engines in German races this year, with a view to a full-scale assault on the 350 cc World Championship in 1955'.

All this was put in jeopardy, however, when the new 1954 125 cc World Champion, Ruppert Hollaus, suffered a fatal accident at Monza while practising for the Italian GP in September. This resulted in the remainder of the NSU team withdrawing from the meeting.

The tragedy was to have far wider implications than anyone could have imagined at the time, for not only did NSU decline to race in Italy, but they also gave the final round, in Spain, a miss, too. Then came the bombshell – in a radio interview, at Stuttgart on 7 October, the managing director of NSU, Dr Gerd Stieler von Heydekampf, said that it was quite possible that the NSU factory would not take an active part in racing during 1955.

He went on to say that this move was under serious consideration and was influenced by two things. Firstly, NSU had been subjected to considerable criticism by a sector of the German press. It was held responsible for the complete elimination of competition and, hence, of interest in racing during 1954. Dr von Heydekampf stated that it was remarkable that, only a few years previously, the same section of the press had been demanding the production of German machines which could compete in international Grand Prix racing and had appealed to NSU to do something about it. Now that NSU had done something that brought success to Germany, the company was being criticized for it. The second 'official' reason was that 'NSU would be devoting much more of its attention to meeting the world demand for more comfortable, more reliable, and cleaner touring machines.'

Another factor put forward, at least by the motorcycling journals of the day, was a possible shortage of good riders with which the Neckarsulm factory would be faced in the following season. This position was made more acute as it was corporate policy to employ only the smallest and lightest jockeys. Not only was Hollaus dead, but Baltisburger had been seriously injured during practice for the German GP at Solitude, while Müller, then turned 45, was reported to be retiring. The same was said of Haas. He was just in the process of entering business as a filling-station proprietor. Haas was the

proud owner of a new service facility on the autobahn near his home town of Augsburg.

Speculation became a reality when, on 22 October 1954, NSU announced that it would not be contesting the following year's World Championship series with a works team.

In part compensation for the void left by the decision not to race the Rennfox or Rennmax, the company announced that it was to market an 'over-the-counter' machine for privateers. This was the Sportmax, and production of this overhead-cam single was to begin in early 1955.

The prototype of what was to emerge as the Sportmax had appeared as early as the end of the

Overleaf
Australian Bob Brown (9) leads 18-year-old Mike Hailwood (18). Both are mounted on NSU Sportmax machines. This 1958 TT battle finished with Hailwood third and Brown fourth

Below
John Surtees amassed a vast number of victories on his Sportmax. He is seen here in winning form at Thruxton in July 1955

1953 season, during the Spanish GP at Montjuich Park, Barcelona. Development had continued throughout that winter. Pre-production examples made their début in May 1954 at Hockenheim, where one finished sixth against world-class opposition.

However, it was not until August 1954 that the new NSU single showed its real potential, when one piloted by Georg Braun finished a superb second behind works rider Hollaus on a Rennmax twin, with Müller, on another of the twins, in third spot.

The development machines were essentially similar to the actual production models, but they employed a smaller-diameter front brake and had other minor changes.

Developed from the production Max roadster, the Sportmax was the work of Karl Kleinbach. However, controversy remains over exactly how many genuine Sportmax machines were built. The NSU publicity officer, Arthur Westrup, stated that it was 17

His fairing showing signs of a spill, Sportmax rider Horst Kassner still managed to secure fourth spot in the 250 cc race at the Nürburgring during the German GP, 20 July 1958

while other, normally reliable, sources put the figure as high as 34. Additionally, a number of other machines were built later from spare parts when the contents of the race shop were sold to the Herz family in the late 1950s.

To add further confusion, a large number of 'replicas' were built from the various Max, Special Max and Super Max machines over the years. Some were extremely well done, but, unfortunately, this was not always the case. The roadster frames, forks and brakes are easily recognized and give these spurious 'replicas' away.

The genuine Sportmax, or Type 251 RS (250 single-cylinder Rennsport) had a capacity of 247 cc (69×66 mm) and a compression ratio of 9.8:1, giving 28 bhp at 9000 rpm (maximum safe revs: 9500 rpm). The piston was a forged three-ring Mahle, and an Amal GP $1\frac{3}{16}$ in. carb was fitted. The distinctive 22-litre tank was fabricated in hand-beaten alloy, and the dry weight was 116 kg (256 lb). Tyre size was 18 in. A wide range of alternative sprockets was available to provide the owner with a choice of gearing. Its near-125 mph maximum speed made it the quickest 250 production racer that money could buy at the time of its introduction.

Alan Dugdale at Church Bends with his Sportmax, Isle of Man TT, 1959. He finished ninth

Compared with the prototypes, which had 180 mm-diameter front brakes, the production examples sported massive 210 mm units. Even though NSU decided against entering their pukka works machinery in the 1955 championship, a Neckarsulm bike still won the coveted 250 cc world title.

Ridden by Hermann Müller, a semi-works Sportmax production racer astounded the racing fraternity by scooping the crown. Müller achieved this outstanding feat by consistent performances, rather than heroics, winning only a single round, the German GP at the Nürburgring. In fact, during the five-round series, besides Müller, there were five separate race victors: Lomas, Taveri, Surtees and Ubbiali.

At the end of the season, Müller and Lomas tied on points, the German only getting the verdict after the Englishman was downgraded, following an incident at the Dutch TT. Müller then retired from racing, after more than 20 years in the sport.

However, this was not the end of the Sportmax. Over the next few years, many riders gained successes with the fleet Neckarsulm singles. These included the likes of John Surtees, Hans Baltisburger, Georg Braun, Pierre Monneret, Bob Brown, Sammy Miller and a certain youngster named Mike Hailwood. Its record was truly outstanding, and it was not until the beginning of the 1960s when first the Italian Aermacchi, and later the two-strokes, finally heralded its decline as the 250 cc privateer racer *par excellence*.

NSU's post-war success, at both factory and private level, was relatively short, but during this time its star shone with a unique brilliance.

Record breaking

In the early 1950s, the NSU factory was the largest and most important of some 100 companies that were producing a vast range of products for a post-war Germany hungry for practical, cheap transport. For a short period, in the middle of the decade – if one counts the sales of the Quickly moped – NSU was the largest manufacturer in the motorcycle world. Against this background, the old established Neckarsulm concern was not only to mount a formidable challenge for Grand Prix honours, but amass a truly amazing number of world speed records.

The start of the company's speed records era came at the end of the 1940s with the appearance of a 500 cc version of the pre-war supercharged twin. Such machines were still allowed in German national events at that time, even though they had been banned from international competition by the FIM in 1946.

NSU soon realized that it had a potential record breaker on its hands when, in May 1950, works rider Heiner Fleischmann had been timed at 143.75 mph at

Above
Wilhelm Herz (with crash helmet) and NSU race shop mechanic Mack inspect the supercharged 500 twin-cylinder machine prior to the successful world speed record attempt in April 1951

Left
Many Max, Special Max and Super Max roadsters were converted into Sportmax replicas. Here is one such machine belonging to L. A. James at Silverstone in 1960. His mechanic, Val Blower, is in the background with the rider's 350 Norton

Hockenheim on the big-bore twin. When one realizes that, in supercharged form, this engine gave almost 100 bhp, it is perhaps easier to understand. (This was *double* what a normally-aspirated works 500 Norton was giving at the time!)

To confirm this potential, Wilhelm Herz broke the world speed record (then held by BMW) with a speed of 180.17 mph, using one of the blown 500 parallel twin engines mounted in a streamlined alloy

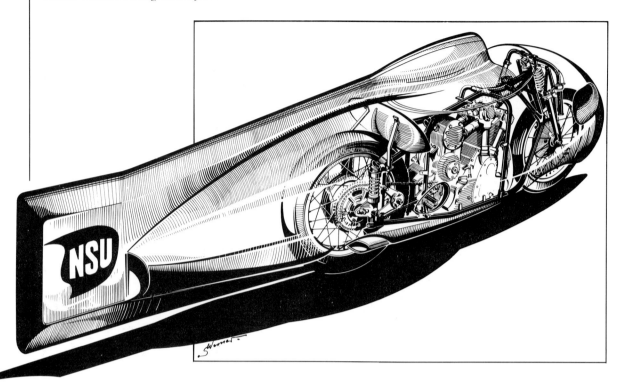

Construction details of the 1951 Herz record-breaker

shell. The venue was the Munich-Ingolstadt auto-bahn and the date, 12 April 1951.

This feat was followed later the same day by Hermann Böhm, on the same machine equipped with a third 'outrigger' wheel, who set a new sidecar record at 154 mph. Even though he had achieved over 180 mph, at the time, Herz said that had a more suitable course been available, then an even higher speed would have been obtainable. The reason was that the part of the autobahn which the team were able to use was not long enough, rather than having an unsuitable surface. The problem centred around the effect two bridges across the autobahn had on the steering of the streamlined machine. So great was the sideways thrust at these points – even on a calm day – that the distance had to be reduced. An unusual facet of the record attempt was that narrow *ribbed* 19 in. tyres were used on both wheels. Besides the 499 cc engine, a 348 cc supercharged unit was also fitted into the chassis to obtain a new world record in this category for the flying kilometre at 172.5 mph. On this run, the engine was over-revved, with the result that valve float caused indentations in the piston crowns to a depth of nearly 2 mm!

The next piece of news concerning NSU and record breaking came shortly after dawn on Tuesday 21 April, 1954, when a bearded commercial artist, named Gustav Adolf Baumm, gained world-wide recognition by breaking a total of 11 small-capacity world speed records with NSU-powered stream-liners designed by himself and built in the Neckar-sulm company's race shop. The most unusual aspect of the Baumm design was that the rider – himself – lay horizontally with his feet forward. As *Motor Cycling* reported in their 29 April 1954 issue, this 'could scarcely have been ideal for the gusty conditions which prevailed.' Various records, at speeds between 79.4 and 111.2 mph were broken in the 50, 75 and 100 cc classes.

For the smaller classes, the engine used was based upon the 49 cc Quickly moped unit, but tuned to produce 3.4 bhp at 7000 rpm. The larger unit was from a 98 cc Sportfox, which provided 7.5 bhp at the same revolutions. Both ran on alcohol fuel, but the main reason for the increased speed was the effec-tiveness of the fish-like alloy streamlining.

The miniature projectiles had disc-type 16 in. wheels, while the suspension, front and rear, was by rubber bands on the Quickly-powered machine, and pneumatic damping on the larger bike. On each machine, both wheels were fitted with brakes. Steering was effected by two levers, one on each side of the reclining rider, and the various controls were fixed to the appropriate levers.

The record venue chosen, once again, was a section of the Munich-Ingolstadt autobahn, near

Above
NSU was able to claim the sidecar speed record as well, thanks to Hermann Böhm, seen here preparing for the attempt

Below
Böhm with the 'sidecar' record-breaker. Essentially, it was the same machine employed for the solo runs, but fitted with an outrigger wheel

Two important figures in the NSU record-breaking story – Gustav Baumm (left) and Dipl. Ing. Walter Froede – discuss tactics in 1954

Munich itself. The weather, it was claimed, ensured that speeds obtained with the smaller engine were lower than had been expected.

However, very much overshadowing these events was the rumour that an attempt would shortly be made to raise the world's maximum to some 200 mph – using the Baumm shell and one of the latest works Rennmax racing twin-cylinder engines.

Originally, Baumm had conceived the idea for his 'flying hammock' record breaker in 1950, when occupied as a draughtsman at the NSU factory. At first, his concept was accepted by only one man. That was the head of the racing department, Dipl. Ing. Froede. After designing the Rennmax, Froede had transferred its development to Ewald Praxl, allowing Baumm's design to be fabricated under the direct supervision of Froede himself. Froede realized the potential of Baumm's concept, not only as a record breaker, but also as the layout for a racing machine of the future and even for every-day touring work.

Readers should realize that Froede had the responsibility not only of overseeing Baumm's project, but also of being directly involved with several other important engineering projects at NSU, including fuel injection, rotary valves, rotary engines (later to emerge as the Wankel), and hydraulic transmission systems. He was a brilliant engineer, but also a very busy one.

By the end of 1954, following the 'lukewarm' official reception of the Baumm concept, the whole of NSU's senior management had decided to back it fully. No doubt, this was helped by the decision, at least for the time being, to retire from Grand Prix racing. To replace the prestige which they felt they would lose through their GP withdrawal, a policy was agreed to attempt to gain speed records not already held by the company. There was a simple policy statement: 'Maximum speed with minimum engine capacity.'

It was apparent that longer distances would be needed if a rider was to accelerate to higher speeds when using low-power outputs, so it was agreed that it would be necessary to travel outside the German borders for the majority of future attempts. The sites chosen were the salt flats in Utah, on the western side of the USA. As early as December 1954,

2.00 × 16 tyres were being laboratory tested up to 240 mph. Throughout the winter of 1954–5, Baumm, Froede and other NSU engineers toiled away on the new breed of record breaker, and the following spring, it was announced that certain world speed categories would be attempted during the period 27 April–5 May 1955. For these, however, the Munich-Ingolstadt autobahn location would be used rather than the salt flats.

Unfortunately, bad weather prevented the record attempt until Tuesday 10 May, when NSU established a total of 22 world records in the 50, 75, 125, 175, 250 and 350 categories – with 50 and 125 cc machines. The records were set by Gustav Baumm, using a pair of streamliners of the same type as those employed in his previous record spree. One machine was fitted with the tuned Quickly-based engine described previously, the other with one of the 1954 123 cc Rennfox works racing engines. Six of the previous records were already held by Baumm, and all the others, save two, were in Italian hands (Ceccato, Lambretta and Moto Guzzi). One of the exceptions was the 75 cc five-mile record, which had been established by the Englishman Hall in 1929 on a Rocket-JAP. No 50 cc figure had previously been created for five miles.

Hermann Müller prepares for a run in one of the Baumm-inspired NSU streamliners, 1955

Müller (left) and Herz at Bonneville while preparing for the record-breaking spree, October 1956

Each of Baumm's NSU's attacked the flying start kilometre, mile, five-kilometre and five-mile distances. The 50 cc machine recorded mean speeds of 93.2, 93.8, 90.4 and 91.3 mph for the respective distances, setting up records in both 50 and 75 cc classes; the margin over the earlier speeds varied from 56.5 mph, in the case of Hall's record, to 9.3 mph for the 75 cc kilometre record. Equally remarkable – perhaps even more so – was the performance of the 125 streamliner in covering the distances at respective mean speeds of 134.8, 135.4, 129.8 and 131.0 mph. The speed brought NSU the appropriate records in the 125, 175 and 250 cc

categories, as well as the 350 cc five-kilometre and five-mile records. The smallest gain was approximately 2.5 mph on the previous 250 cc kilometre speed, whereas Baumm's old five-mile 125 speed was bettered by nearly 24 mph.

Later, at a dinner party for delegates to the FIM congress in Düsseldorf, given by the NSU management on Thursday 12 May, Baumm was guest of honour. One of his record machines was also on show, together with the two engines used in the successful attempt.

There were distinct differences between the two streamliners used. The smaller-engined machine was higher and shorter than the larger-engined model; the latter had a less-rounded top to its shell. There were good reasons for these differences, for although Baumm was officially described as an artist, in fact, he was a highly-skilled designer in his own right, who had been employed on aircraft development during the war. So carefully had Baumm worked out the contours of his 'feet-first' machines, that even with a gusty 12 mph side-wind blowing, the steering during the record attempts 'was unaffected'. Baumm suggested that the flatter shell of the 125 might be thought to have been aimed at keeping the front wheel on the road. However, he revealed that experience had shown that as the speed rose, so more weight was transferred to the *front* wheel, to such an extent that very powerful springs had to be incorporated in the front suspension of the larger model. On the day of the successful attempts, the wind had been blowing so hard that Baumm claimed to have lost around 500 rpm from the maximum figures for both engines in preliminary testing.

The unsupercharged dohc Rennfox engine employed fuel injection. Originally, there had been plans to run it on alcohol, but the performance characteristics of these units, when using premium-grade petrol, were so exactly determined and documented that NSU technicians decided to rely upon the known, rather than introduce an element of experimentation. When asked about the safe limit at which his streamliner could be navigated, Baumm estimated 'about 150 mph', but revealed that a similar design, built for higher speeds, might be able to approach 300 mph if propelled by a 500 cc engine. A little-known fact was that Baumm was then in the process of designing a four-wheeled passenger vehicle embodying some of the aerodynamic features of this record breaker. However, this was a private venture without the support of NSU.

Sadly, a mere 11 days after the Düsseldorf dinner, on Monday 23 May, disaster struck – Baumm was killed when testing a prototype of the streamliner with which it was planned that NSU would make a comeback in the 1956 125 and 250 Grands Prix. Baumm was track testing this machine at the Nürburgring and in mixed company, including Porsche cars, when he lost control and ran off the circuit into some trees. He suffered a fractured skull and died from his injuries. So ended the dreams of the bearded 36-year-old Bavarian. Moreover, many of NSU's future plans were to take a totally different course than would have been the case otherwise.

Baumm was not only developing the machine that was to be the basis for NSU's racing comeback, but also a series of production versions that were to have precise handling, improved speed and dramatically better fuel consumption for any given capacity. The company received a bad press over the Baumm accident and, as it turned out, this was to influence its very future. The whole project was shelved, and thereafter, NSU concentrated on other things, notably a return to car production.

All that remains of the Baumm era today is one of his machines, owned by the Herz family, in the new Hockenheim-ring Museum. This machine is actually the later one used by Müller in his endurance/fuel consumption trials at the 'Ring' in May 1956. This was one of the shelved racers, shorter than the record machine, longer than the proposed roadster. It is rumoured that a shell from one of the record breakers exists, too.

Following record sales in 1955 (NSU produced more powered two-wheelers that year than anyone else in the world), came the first news, at the beginning of July, that 1956 was not continuing this trend, and NSU announced that 640 workers were to be dismissed over the following two months, owing to sales being lower than expected. At the same time, reports filtered through that more record attempts were in the wind, testing being carried out on the same section of the autobahn again.

Hermann Müller was there with 'Baumm II', a revised version of Gustav Baumm's original Rennfox-powered streamliner, while Wilhelm Herz had the 'Delphin III', the latest version of the 1951 record breaker. This had a completely-redesigned form of streamlining, with enclosed cabin, nose window, taller tail fin and various other changes which, like those on the smaller machine, had been developed in the Stuttgart Technical College wind tunnel. The result was a cut in the drag co-efficient from 0.29, in its original form, to 0.19. With its 110 bhp supercharged engine, NSU claimed that the rehashed twin could better 125 mph in *first* gear.

Another version of the Baumm-type machine had a Rennmax 250 racing twin GP engine unit installed, fulfilling the dream of the late Gustav Baumm who, together with Dr Froede, had planned this very machine.

The purpose of the testing was a massive effort to wrest the maximum number of world records, and to this effect, no expense was spared. The venue was to be the Bonneville Salt Flats, Utah, in the USA. Accompanying the tri-coloured machines (they were

Overleaf
Herz and 'Delphin III' on Bonneville salt flats after his successful record-breaking run. It brought the curtain down on a period of NSU achievement in several forms of motorcycle sport

Below
The cockpit of Wilhelm Herz's 'Delphin III', on which he achieved a new motorcycle speed record at 210.64 mph in 1956

red on top, white in the middle and blue-grey below to make them easily visible against the salt) was a party of 30, including timing experts from the Longines factory. The riders were to be Herz and Müller, while Werner Haas went as a reserve rider.

On 29 July, a day before the full record-breaking feast was due to start, Herz and Müller made some experimental runs, which were not claimed as records. Herz, with the 350 supercharged twin, bettered 180 mph for both the kilometre and mile, and clocked over 182 mph on the five-kilometre and five-mile runs, while Müller, with a 125, was close to 140 mph in both the kilometre and mile dashes.

Herz also took a turn on the unblown 250 Baumm Special. Reported to have been travelling at a speed in excess of 200 mph, he was struck by a blast of wind from the side which overturned the machine. Amazingly, he escaped with no more than bruises, but the damage to the shell was enough to retire it from any further use. The Rennmax engine was then transferred to a more conventional streamliner for further record attempts.

Rain having made the surface of the lake tricky, the programme was delayed until Wednesday 1 August. Knowing that the capabilities of the 350 had not been reached, Herz again ran this machine, while Müller was to make a repeat performance on the 125. On the return run for the first round trip of the day, Herz was again plagued with problems, this time hitting a patch of wet salt which veered him far enough off the course to wipe out a timing-light stand. Fortunately, he was still able to return to the pits under the machine's own power. Damage to the nose needed repairing and, in any case, the still-damp surface prevented any further attempts by Müller for the balance of the day.

The next day, 2 August, Herz set the following flying-start 350 cc records: kilometre, 188.5 mph; mile, 189.5 mph; five-kilometre, 183 mph. On the same day, Müller took out the 125 Baumm-type machine to claim the following flying-start records (all of which stood to the late Gustav Baumm): kilometre, 150 mph; mile, 150.78 mph; five-kilometre, 148.5 mph; five-mile, 149 mph.

Then, two days later, on Saturday 4 August, came the big one, a new world's fastest motorcycle speed was achieved when Herz, the 46-year-old from Ludwigshaven, rocketed his flying, enclosed, super-charged, 500 parallel twin over the Bonneville Salt Flats to an amazing two-way average of 210.64 mph.

This represented a 25 mph increase over the existing record set by Russell Wright in New Zealand, on 2 July 1955, with an unblown, 998 cc Vincent V-twin. It was also 18 mph faster than the *unofficial* 192 mph record established by American Johnny Allen with a 649 cc Triumph-engined, cigar-shaped streamliner on 25 September 1955. Also that day, four 100 cc flying-start records were set by Müller, following Herz's successful run, using a 'Baumm II' machine powered by a stroked and sleeved down racing Rennfox unit (99.7 cc, 56×40.5 mm, 15.5 bhp at 11,000 rpm): kilometre, 137.86 mph; mile, 137.86 mph, five-kilometre, 136.62 mph; five-mile, 137.24 mph.

Strong winds then caused more record attempts to be cancelled for a couple of days. When these were resumed, Müller broke the standing ten-mile, two-way average with a speed of 151 mph in the 125 streamliner. On the blown, 49 cc, two-stroke unit, he averaged 119 mph over the flying mile, and with the 250 Rennmax engine in the 'Delphin III', Herz averaged 152 mph over the same distance.

When all the dust had settled, NSU was to claim a total of 54 new records. Besides the obvious outright speed record, the most noteworthy was the bettering of the ten-kilometre and ten-mile *350 cc*-class records by the 'Baumm II' streamliner powered by a 125 Rennfox engine. Since the existing figures had been set in the previous October by Dickie Dale with a 350 Guzzi works racer, the NSU performance deserved high praise.

With the marathon American record session over, the team returned to Germany; the last chapter of NSU's glorious post-war speed effort had ended. Then the machines were sent on a world-wide tour to gain the maximum amount of publicity.

At the time, this was badly needed, as the press was carrying headlines like: 'German Industry Slowing'. There were reports that from September 1 NSU had started a 36-hour week because of slack trade. Following so quickly from the large dismissal of workers in July, this was a clear warning that all was not sweetness and light in Neckarsulm.

Although, unlike the majority, NSU survived the mass of closures throughout 1956–8, the German motorcycle industry was destined never to recover from the golden days of the early post-war period. That fling of record breaking was to prove NSU's swan-song and the pinnacle of its motorcycle achievements. Truly, it was the end of a golden era.

13
Simson – not only mopeds

The beginnings of the Simson marque can be traced back to 1856, when its predecessor, the Ernst Thalmann Hunting Weapon Works, began manufacturing armaments in the East German town of Suhl, in the Thuringian Forest.

Like several other manufacturers of arms, the Suhl company needed to diversify during the times when armaments were no longer in demand. Together with Puch in Austria, FN in Belgium, Husqvarna in Sweden and, of course, BSA in Britain, the German concern needed to put its manufacturing machinery to work in peacetime. So all of them turned to building that basic form of transport, the pedal cycle.

The Suhl factory began to turn out bicycles in 1896, and even these were innovative for their day. They were fitted with pneumatic tyres when much of Europe was still having its bones shaken.

However, whereas many bicycle manufacturers made the transition into motorcycle production, the

East German concern moved into cars. It was in this new field that the name Simson-Supra first appeared, under which various forms of touring and light sporting vehicles were offered until the mid 1930s.

The company then reverted to making two-wheelers, at first with pedal power. Later, in 1938, it began production, under the name Mofa, of 98 cc, Sachs-engined, ultra-lightweight motorcycles.

With the intervention of World War 2 in the following year, and the partitioning of Germany in the aftermath, it was late 1952 before the former Jadgwaffen werke resumed powered two-wheeler production once more.

First of the new models was the SR-1, a very basic moped with a two-speed gearbox. Its 47.6 cc engine

The 250 AWO (Simson) ohv single on which Rudolf Juhrich finished 18th in the 1954 German Grand Prix at Solitude

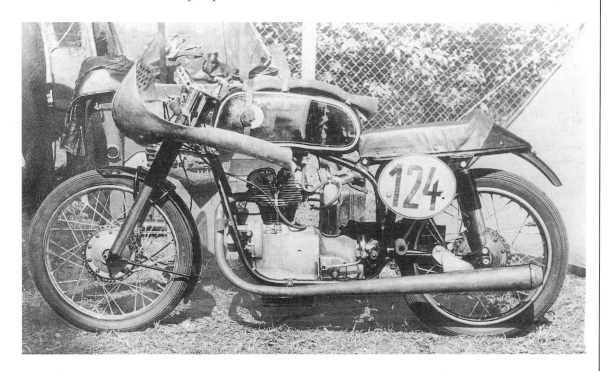

Hans Weinert, East German 250 cc Champion in both 1958 and 1959, on his Simson RS. The factory then switched its efforts to long-distance trials

developed 1.3 bhp and provided just enough power for it to reach 30 mph. The specification was completed by 26 in. wheels and rubber suspension at both front and rear.

Sold under the AWO label, the SR-1 was very similar to the West German NSU Quickly in both appearance and design concept. It was followed, soon afterwards, by the improved SR-2, which proved instantly popular and went on to become the biggest seller of all among East German two-wheelers in the 1950s and early 1960s.

Building on the success of these ventures, the company's next model was the AWO 425, with a 250 ohv engine. This featured a vertically-mounted cylinder, the crankshaft sitting longitudinally in the frame. The configuration naturally led to the adoption of shaft drive, via a four-speed gearbox.

Initially, power output was a lowly 12 bhp at 5500 rpm. Running on a compression ratio of 6:5:1, the machine could be ordered in either solo or sidecar guise, each with its own set of gear ratios.

The AWO 425 closely resembled both the BMW R25 series and the Swiss Universal. It was typically Germanic with its separate, sprung saddles and plunger rear suspension.

In a market that was ever hungry for an improved means of transport, the AWO 250 single soon found its way into competition, both on and off-road. For the 1954 racing season, the factory developed a tuned version to contest the East German road-racing championships.

The first racer managed to be reasonably successful, even though it retained the roadster's pushrod-operated valves, engine-speed clutch and shaft drive. However, by the time Rudolph Jurich rode an AWO to 18th position in the German Grand Prix, during July 1954, the design sported swinging-arm rear suspension and a duplex frame.

There then followed a considerable amount of experimentation with the works racers, especially in the engine and final-drive departments. Some machines were tried with single- and double-overhead-camshaft heads. Various methods of valve actuation were tested, including bevel drive, a train of gears, and chain drive to the cams. There was even an experimental twin-cylinder double-knocker.

The results came thick and fast, the Suhl factory

taking the national championships three years running in the quarter-litre category: 1954, 1955 and 1956. Moreover, although it only ever contested the German Grand Prix in the World Championship series, several finishes were recorded, including a 15th place in 1955.

The track successes brought a demand for a more sporting version of the road-going 425. This was coded 425S (Sport). The engine was the familiar pushrod 247 cc single, but with the power bumped up to 14 bhp at 6300 rpm, providing a maximum speed of over 70 mph. Although shaft drive was retained, the frame was totally redesigned. This was quite innovative for its time, being of pressed-steel with some components of tubular construction. For its day, the result was a machine of exceptionally clean lines.

Even so, it was the much cheaper, two-stroke commuter model which provided the factory with the vast majority of its profit. Luckily, this did not halt development of the four-stroke racing programme. The next machine to appear – and, as it happened, the definitive model – was the RS (Renn Sport) 250, which made its début in early 1958.

By now, AWO had given way to Simson, and with the capable Hans Weinert aboard, the newcomer took many honours, including the national titles in both 1958 and 1959. Although rarely seen in the West, the Simson RS250 was state-of-the-art when it appeared. Its specification included chain-driven,

double overhead camshafts, full unit-construction, dry clutch, six-speed gearbox, alloy tanks (it had a dry sump) and a full, hand-beaten, alloy dolphin fairing. The forks were of the leading-link type, while braking was taken care of by a pair of massive, full-width alloy hubs, there being a two-leading-shoe arrangement at the front.

One RS250 was raced in the 1959 German GP at Hockenheim, where it displayed a fair turn of speed against the very latest Italian machinery, such as the MV twins and the Morini single. However, with the last of the four-stroke roadsters rolling off the Suhl production line in 1960, the time had come for the Simson road-racing challenge to be brought to an end.

This was due to two factors. The first was that two-strokes had taken over well and truly in the communist bloc behind the 'Iron Curtain'. Perhaps the most important of all, however, was that the East German motorcycle industry had been rationalized under the auspices of the IFA (Industrieverband-Farhzuegebau). MZ (see Chapter 11) was to produce the larger-capacity machines, while Simson was to manufacture bikes with a maximum capacity of 100 cc.

Both companies survive as separate marques today, the marketing pattern being unchanged after 30 years. However, with great reforms taking place within Germany as this is being written, the situation may well change in the near future.

Index